Introduction

This guide features forty circular walks in the Southern Highlands. It includes all of the Munros (peaks above 914m/3000ft) and many Corbetts (peaks over 762m/2500ft), as well as other hills that combine to make good circuits.

Routes have been chosen according to a number of factors, including variety of terrain, great views, historical interest, minimal road walking and the feasibility of a circular route.

Environmental factors such as the ability of access points to support additional cars and opportunities for bypassing visitor-sensitive or eroded areas have also been taken into account. Circular routes help to take the pressure off badly eroded paths, and walking in areas where there have been fewer footsteps is more conducive to natural regeneration of the land.

Walkers can also minimise their own impact on the environment by using purpose-built paths whenever possible and walking in single file to help prevent widening scars. Restricting your use of bikes to tracks, parking sensibly, avoiding fires and litter, and keeping dogs on a lead, particularly on grazing land and during lambing, all help to preserve the land and good relations with its inhabitants. Many of the responsibilities for walkers are now enshrined in law.

How to use this guide

The routes in this book are divided into five regions. These divisions largely represent points of access into the mountains, or use natural geographical boundaries. The opening section for each of the five regions introduces the area, its towns, topography and key features, and contains brief route outlines. It is supplemented by a road map, locating the walks.

Each route begins with an introduction identifying the names and heights of significant tops, the relevant Ordnance Survey (OS) map, total distance and average time. Some routes also contain an option for cycling part of the way where there is a long low-level approach.

A sketch map shows the main topographical details of the area and the route. The map is intended only to give the reader an idea of the terrain, and should not be followed for navigation.

Every route has an estimated round-trip time: this is for rough guidance only and should help in planning, especially when daylight hours are limited. In winter or after heavy rain, extra time should also be added for difficulties underfoot.

Risks and how to avoid them

Many of the hills in this guide are remote and craggy, and the weather in Scotland can change suddenly, reducing visibility to several yards. Winter walking brings particular challenges, including limited daylight, white-outs, cornices and avalanches. Every year, walkers and climbers die from falls or hypothermia in the Scottish mountains. Equally, though, overstretched Mountain Rescue teams are often called out to walkers who are simply tired or hungry.

Preparation for a walk should begin well before you set out, and your choice of route should reflect your fitness, the conditions underfoot and the regional weather forecasts.

None of the walks in this guide should be attempted without the relevant OS Map or equivalent at 1:50,000 (or 1:25,000) and a compass.

Even in summer, warm, waterproof clothing is advisable and footwear that is comfortable and supportive with good grips a must. Don't underestimate how much food and water you need and remember to take any medication required, including reserves in case of illness or delay. Many walkers also carry a whistle, first aid kit and survival bag.

It is a good idea to leave a route description with a friend or relative in case a genuine emergency arises: you should not rely on a mobile phone to get you out of difficulty. If walking as part of a group, make sure your companions are aware of any medical conditions, such as diabetes, and how to deal with problems that may occur.

There is a route for most levels of fitness in this guide, but it is important to know your limitations. Even for an experienced walker, colds, aches and pains can turn an easy walk into an ordeal.

These routes assume some knowledge of navigation in the hills with use of map and compass, though these skills are not difficult to learn. Use of Global Positioning System (GPS) devices is becoming more common but, while GPS can help pinpoint your location on the map in zero visibility, it cannot tell you where to go next.

Techniques such as scrambling or climbing on rock, snow and ice are required on just a few mountains in this guide. Such skills will improve confidence and the ease with which any route can be completed. They will also help you to avoid or escape potentially dangerous areas if you lose your way. The Mountaineering Council of Scotland provides training and information.

For most of these routes, proficiency in walking and map-reading is sufficient.

Access

Until the Land Reform (Scotland) Act was introduced early in 2003, the 'right to roam' in Scotland was a result of continued negotiations between government bodies, interest groups and landowners.

In many respects, the Act simply reinforces the common law right of access to the countryside of Scotland for recreational purposes. However, a key difference is that under the Act the right of access depends on whether it is exercised responsibly.

Landowners have a legal duty not to put up fences, walls or signs that prevent recreational users from crossing their land, but walkers should also take responsibility for their actions when exercising their right of access. Keep to paths and tracks where possible and, if in doubt, ask. At certain times of the year there are special restrictions, both at low level and on the hills, and these should be respected. Signs are usually posted at popular access points with details: there should be no expectation of a right of access to all places at all times.

The right of access does not extend to use of motor vehicles on private or estate roads.

Seasonal restrictions
Red and Sika deer stalking:
Stags: 1 July to 20 October
Hinds: 21 October to 15 February
Deer may also be culled at other times for welfare reasons. The seasons for Fallow and Roe deer (less common) are also longer. Many estates belong to the Hillphones network which provides advance notice of shoots.
Grouse shooting:
12 August to 10 December
Forestry:
Felling: all year
Planting: November to May
Heather burning:
September to April
Lambing:
March to May (Dogs should be kept on a lead at all times near livestock.)

Glossary
Common Gaelic words found in the text and maps:

abhainn	river
ailean	field; grassy plain
àirigh	summer hill pasture; shieling
allt	burn; stream
àth	ford
bàn	white
beag	small
bealach	pass; gap; gorge
beinn	ben; mountain
bràighe	neck; upper part
cìoch	breast; hub; pointed rock
clach	boulder; stone
cnoc	hillock
coire	corrie; cauldron; mountain hollow
creachann	exposed rocky summit
creag	cliff
cruach	heap; stack
dubh	black; dark
garbh	thick; coarse; rough
lagan	hollow; dimple
learg	hillside exposed to sea or sun
lochan	small loch; pool
meall	mound; lump; bunch
mór	big; great; tall
sgòrr	peak; cliff; sharp point
sgùrr	large conical hill
stùc	pinnacle; precipice; steep rock

Glen Lyon is an isolated valley stretching for more than 40km and largely bypassed by the tourist trail. The Romans were early visitors, however, and it is reputed to have been the birthplace of Pontius Pilate.

An adventurous road winds from Fortingall at the eastern end to the mountain-locked west. From the village, the journey into Glen Lyon snakes through a steep gorge and a rich tapestry of native forest. The glen at its widest is a fertile plain with a famous horseshoe of peaks to the north and the Ben Lawers massif to the south.

Bridge of Balgie is at the centre of Glen Lyon. Here the road forks south to the Ben Lawers Nature Reserve and beyond to Killin, and west into the higher reaches of the glen. The upper glen holds two reservoirs, Loch an Daimh, hidden to the north, and Loch Lyon, at the very end of the road.

This section includes four routes that start within the glen, two that begin at the nature reserve, and one that involves peaks on the Glen Lyon watershed but is

reached from Loch Rannoch. Schiehallion is also featured. Although it sits between Loch Rannoch and the River Lyon, this peak is by convention grouped with the Glen Lyon hills. The mountains at the far end and on the southern flanks of Loch Lyon are described elsewhere in this guide.

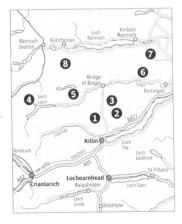

Glen Lyon

The Tarmachan Ridge

Meall nan Tarmachan Ⓜ (1044m),
Meall Garbh (1026m), **Beinn nan Eachan**,
(1000m), **Creag na Caillich** (916m)

Walk time 5h Height gain 900m
Distance 13km OS Map Landranger 51

**A justifiably popular ridge walk with
easy access and good paths in some
exciting terrain. Scrambling skills will
add to confidence on exposed sections.**

Start from the track 800m northwest of
the National Trust for Scotland Visitor
Centre (GR604383). Follow this southwest
to a stile, and take the path on the right
300m beyond. This path rises steadily west
and crosses a fence; thereafter it follows the
ridge north. Climb to the first small top,
dipping to a fence and then climbing
steeply via a small gully to the summit of
Meall nan Tarmachan (GR585390) (2h).
Care should be taken on the ridge as the
cliffs, particularly on the southern and
eastern aspects, are very steep. From the
summit, walk south for about 100m before
bearing southwest along the undulating
ridge to reach the spiky top of Meall Garbh.
From here, the ridge becomes very narrow
with a sudden, tricky descent to a bealach.
The terrain rises gently as you leave the
bealach in a westerly direction. Pass or
climb smaller mounds before ascending
the rounder summit of Beinn nan Eachan

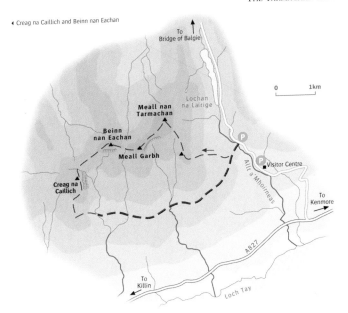

◄ Creag na Caillich and Beinn nan Eachan

(GR570384) (3h). Descend 500m over gentle ground to another bealach. Climb southwest to the last peak where several points compete for the top of Creag na Caillich. The final ascent involves an airy traverse above a big drop. Descend southwards for 700m before the path veers southwest to avoid more cliffs. After reaching flatter ground, the path doubles back over a small bealach and down to a track by a weir. This leads back to the start point (5h).

The National Trust for Scotland

Founded in 1931 to manage and promote public access to sites of historical and natural importance, the National Trust for Scotland maintains castles, houses, gardens and countryside across Scotland. The southern slopes of the Ben Lawers massif and much of the Tarmachan range are owned by the Trust, and the visitor centre at Ben Lawers demonstrates its local activities of habitat restoration, wildlife protection and promoting public access. The area is known for its rare arctic-alpine plants as well as being home to ptarmigan, red grouse, dipper and curlew.

Ben Lawers

Beinn Ghlas Ⓜ (1103m), **Ben Lawers** Ⓜ
(1214m), **An Stùc** Ⓜ(1118m), **Meall
Garbh**Ⓜ(1118m), **Meall Greigh**Ⓜ(1001m)

Walk time 8h Height gain 1500m
Distance 20km OS Map Landranger 51

**A classic ridge combining the highest
peaks of the Southern Highlands.
This is a long excursion with a short
tricky section of descent from An Stùc.**

Start from the National Trust for Scotland
Visitor Centre (GR608379). Follow signs
north for Ben Lawers through a fenced area
shared with a nature trail. After gaining
steady height for 1km, the path exits the
reserve and climbs steepening slopes to the
south ridge of Beinn Ghlas. Follow this ridge
to the summit. Drop down on the prominent
northeast ridge to a bealach, and then
climb steeply to the summit of Ben Lawers
(GR635414) (3h). Descend the pronounced
north ridge, which gives great views into
the eastern corrie. Climb Creag an Fhithich
and down to another bealach. Follow the
south ridge of An Stùc to the summit. Care
is needed when descending this peak on
the northern side: the path drops down over
slabs where you need to use your hands,
but the difficulties are short-lived and the
climb to the summit of Meall Garbh much
easier (GR644436) (4h20). Here, the
character of the ridge changes dramatically
from steep scree and rock to rolling heather
and bog. Accompany the fenceline
eastwards, crossing it by stiles to a marshy
bealach, then follow the path over a chain
of small mounds to the summit of Meall
Greigh (GR674438). Descend southwest and
cross the Lawers Burn at the dam to gain
the end of a water catchment track.
[Escape: a path descends southeast to
Lawers.] Follow the track southwest for
about 4km until it begins a zigzag descent.
After the first switchback, drop towards the

◀ Ben Lawers from across Loch Tay

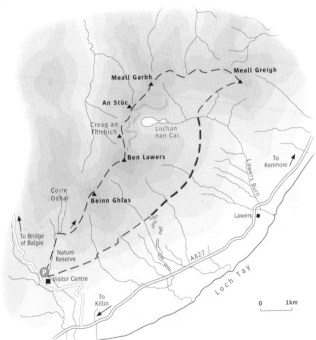

burn where a series of old walls run southwest for around 3km. Keep close to the line of the broken walls: this section can be rough underfoot. Climb around the ridge, and the visitor centre comes into view (8h).

Early cartography

Following the defeat of the Jacobite Rebellion of 1745-6, the Board of Ordnance commissioned a military survey of Scotland to strengthen control of the Highlands. Named after the general who oversaw the project, 'Roy's Map' took eight years to complete and the original hand-drawn result can be viewed in the British Library. On Ben Lawers, traces of a base used for early mapping can be found about 250m ESE of the summit.

Along Glen Lyon to the old ruins

Meall a'Choire Léith Ⓜ(926m),
Meall Corranaich Ⓜ(1069m)

Walk time 8h20 Height gain 1000m
Distance 24km OS Map Landranger 51

A demanding circuit in the highest massif of the Southern Highlands, taking in two peaks and descending through an historic glen.

Start on the south side of the bridge in Bridge of Balgie (GR576467). (Park south of the village beyond the cattle grid.) Take the track signposted for the Meggernie Outdoor Activities Centre (often used by the Scout Association) just south of the bridge. Ignore the first turning for the centre and continue eastwards along the track for about 3.5km,

passing through several gates, until you reach a long cattle shed and two white farmhouses. Immediately opposite the houses there is an old grassy track, which climbs south by a burn. After 1.5km of gentle ascent, cross the burn by a footbridge and pass over another track to ascend steep grassy slopes eastwards, keeping to the south side of a wall until you reach the ridgeline. Follow the ridge south: this is steep at first before easing off towards the summit of Meall a'Choire Léith (GR613439) (3h40). Descend south to a bealach, and then keep to the east of a tiny burn. Maintain the high ground to reach the pronounced ridge which leads to the summit of Meall Corranaich (GR615410)

(5h). Descend steeply ESE to a bealach shared with Beinn Ghlas. Drop down on the north side and watch for an old track, now grassed over, that zigzags down the west side of the corrie. The track ends at the confluence of two burns. Continue your descent through the glen for several kilometres, passing old ruins, a dam and some shielings before coming to a fence and more ruins. From here, a good track leads to another large white house where it meets the original track. Follow this west through the gates and back to Bridge of Balgie (8h20).

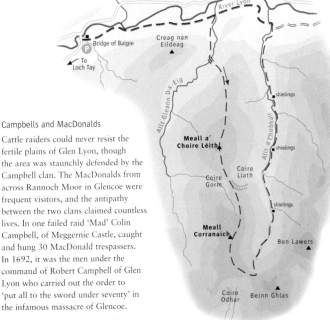

Campbells and MacDonalds

Cattle raiders could never resist the fertile plains of Glen Lyon, though the area was staunchly defended by the Campbell clan. The MacDonalds from across Rannoch Moor in Glencoe were frequent visitors, and the antipathy between the two clans claimed countless lives. In one failed raid 'Mad' Colin Campbell, of Meggernie Castle, caught and hung 30 MacDonald trespassers. In 1692, it was the men under the command of Robert Campbell of Glen Lyon who carried out the order to 'put all to the sword under seventy' in the infamous massacre of Glencoe.

◀ Glen Lyon's northern peaks from Gleann Da-Eig

13

The Yellow Hill

Meall Daill (869m), **Meall Buidhe** Ⓒ (910m)

Walk time 5h40 Height gain 900m
Distance 15km OS Map Landranger 51

A quiet walk at the end of Glen Lyon with views over Rannoch Moor to Glencoe and the Mamores.

   Start just west of the tiny hamlet of Pubil at a bridge 600m before the dam (GR459419). A gravel track leads from the north side of the river and immediately forks. Take the left fork over the gate and away from the farm buildings, climbing steeply west until you are above the dam. Continue west on the north side of the loch for about 4km to a bridge over the Eas Eoghannan. Just after the bridge, watch for a small track on the right which comes immediately to a gate. Pass through the gate to ascend the broad grassy flanks of Meall Daill directly northwest to the summit (GR413434) (2h40). Descend

northwest and follow the ridge to a quaggy bealach shared with Meall na Féith' Faide. Instead of climbing this, contour northeast to join fenceposts. Follow these east over rockier terrain to the summit of Meall Buidhe (Yellow Hill) (GR427450) (4h). To descend, arc east and then south by the fenceposts, or drop directly southeast: both take you to a bealach. Climb eastwards to gain another undulating top with a tiny lochan. Descend southeast along a good ridge over Meall Phubuill. Lower down, keep to the west side of the fence to emerge on the original track. From here, it is a short distance back to the start (5h40).

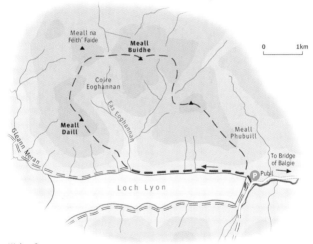

The Hielan Coo

These animals thrive in the harshest of conditions: high rainfall, strong winds and poor grazing. They have two coats: a permanent light under-down and a coarser outer layer, which grows in autumn and recedes by the summer. The cows maintain a herd hierarchy and only look aggressive if they think their calves or leader are threatened. A mature bull can weigh 800kg in its prime, and a cow 500kg. They can live to 18 years and during that time a mother may breed 15 calves. It is not known how well they can see through their fringes.

◄ Looking westwards along Loch Lyon

Above Loch an Daimh

Sròn Chona Choirein (927m),
Stuchd an Lochain ⓜ(960m)

Walk time 3h40 Height gain 600m
Distance 9km OS Map Landranger 51

A short route which starts high and offers fine views of the peaks around the upper end of Glen Lyon.

Start at the end of the road below the dam of Loch an Daimh (GR510464). Cross the bridge and follow the road to the top of the southern side of the dam where it becomes a track. There is a fence on the left. Follow this for 50m until it turns east. Climb southwards on the left of a shallow bowl towards a band of cliffs, passing these on the right to reach a flat area. Continue your climb to pick up the east ridge of Creag an Fheadain, and follow a line of fenceposts to the top. Descend to the southwest, and then rise slightly to the top of Sròn Chona Choirein. Follow the fenceline westwards over undulating ground to the summit of Stuchd an Lochain (GR483448) (2h20). Descend a prominent ridge due north towards the loch. This is sometimes steep, with exposure on the corrie side, but never difficult. Further down, the ridge loses definition but continue down grassy slopes to reach the shore of the loch by clumps of trees. Head east along the loch over occasionally boggy terrain: this leads to a boathouse and a track which takes you back to the start (3h40).

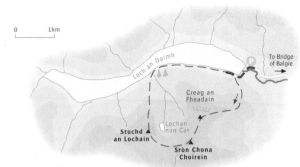

Hydroelectricity

Lochs an Daimh and Giorra were joined in the 1950s by a dam built to harness hydro-electric power. It is part of the Breadalbane Scheme which catches and pipes water over a large area from Glen Lyon to St Fillans. Water is piped south to the Stronuich Reservoir and on to the power station in Glen Lochay. Between 1945 and 1975, Scottish engineers built 50 major dams and power stations, 400 miles of road and over 20,000 miles of power line, overcoming the many geological difficulties of the Highlands.

▼ Upper Glen Lyon

The Glen Lyon Horseshoe

Carn Gorm Ⓜ(1029m), **Meall Garbh** Ⓜ
(968m), **Carn Mairg** Ⓜ(1041m),
Meall na Aighean Ⓜ(981m)

Walk time 7h Height gain 1300m
Distance 17km OS Map Landranger 51

**A well-known circuit which climbs four
summits in quick succession with great
views over the lower glen.**

   Start at the large gate opposite the phone
box in Invervar (GR666483). (Parking is
limited here, so park 800m west.) Beyond
the gate, a track leads north through a
wood. When it emerges from the trees, this
follows the Invervar Burn northwards before
diminishing to a path. Cross the burn above
the plantation and head west up gradually
steepening slopes. These become the
southeast ridge of Carn Gorm which then
leads to the summit (GR635502) (3h).
Descend via the northeast ridge, contour
around the north side of An Sgorr to a
bealach, and climb to the undulating tops
of Meall Garbh. Bear east past a small

lochan, and follow the high ground and twisted iron fences to Meall a'Bhàrr. Continue east: a path rises gently on the south side of Carn Mairg to its unusual rocky top (GR684513) (5h). Descend steep slopes on the eastern side, then drop south to a bealach. Climb south to the top of Meall na Aighean and walk to its eastern

summit (GR695497). Return to the west top, descend north for about 300m in distance and then follow the increasingly pronounced west ridge down towards Roinn na Creige. This is a long section which is occasionally steep, but the ridge eventually joins the track at the edge of the forest. Follow this back to the road (7h).

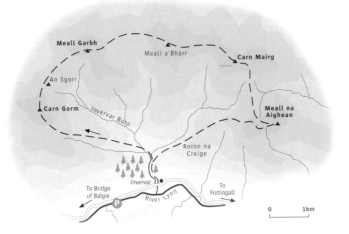

Galar Mhór

Carn Mairg, high above Glen Lyon, translates as 'hill of sorrow' or 'hill of the dead'. The name refers to the *Galar Mhór*, a plague that swept through the glen in the 7th century. St Adamnan, known locally as St Eonan, is attributed with halting the plague and saving the lives of the Glen Lyon people by praying for a miracle. He returned to Glen Lyon in old age and was buried at Dull, near Aberfeldy. He was also the biographer of St Columba of Iona, where he was an Abbot, and St Adamnan's Day is celebrated on 23 September.

◄ Evening mist in Glen Lyon from Meall na Aighean

Schiehallion

Schiehallion Ⓜ (1083m)

Walk time 4h20 Height gain 800m
Distance 9km OS Map Landranger 51 or 52

A celebrated peak owned by the John Muir Trust. Footpath rebuilding and conservation has reduced erosion and improved the route to the top.

Start from the Braes of Foss car park (GR752557). From the south end of the car park, follow the path southwest over moorland to reach a set of old ruins after 1km. Beyond the ruins, the path begins to zigzag westwards to gain considerable height, and then follows the main east ridge which becomes more defined as it rises. Continue west on the long shoulder of the mountain, ascending several false summits and passing numerous cairns. Small quartzite boulders give way to larger blocks towards the summit at the far end of the ridge (GR714547) (2h40). Return down the east ridge, passing a stone circle after 800m and dropping sharply for a short

distance. Cross a broad, flat area for 300m, passing more cairns. Leave the ridge by descending NNE over a short section of fairly steep scree and grass. From here, bear northeast over gently folding terrain towards the heathery knoll of Cnoc nan Aighean and its small cairn. Descend east, following a vague ridge and undulating heather towards two clumps of old pine and the farmhouse of Braes of Foss. Follow a fence to the road: turn right and make the short walk back to the start (4h20).

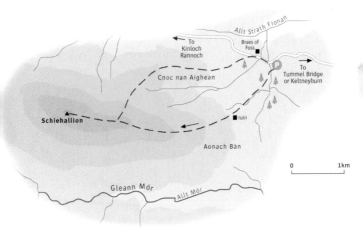

The Attraction of Mountains

Astronomer Royal, the Reverend Nevil Maskelyne, camped out for four months on Schiehallion in 1774 to gauge the density of the Earth. The mountain had been selected for its symmetry and isolation, and Maskelyne measured the deflection of a weight away from the vertical caused by the mass of the peak. This tested a theorem known as the Attraction of Mountains, devised by Isaac Newton in 1687. The team endured considerable hardship on the mountain, alleviated by plenty of whisky brought up from Perth. At the end of their time there, they threw a wild party which ended with their bothy burning to the ground.

◂ Schiehallion from Loch Kinardochy

21

The Secluded Glen

Meall Buidhe m (932m),
Cam Chreag c (862m)

Walk time 8h20 Height gain 900m
Distance 24km OS Map Landranger 51

A long moorland circuit in peaceful, less visited hills on the edge of Rannoch Moor. The route returns by a hidden tree-lined ravine.

Start from the track 20m south of the Georgetown Primary School in Bridge of Gaur (GR504565). (On schooldays, park by a wide gravel track just north of the school.) The track, which is marked for the Finnart Estate, rises gently south into the flatlands beyond. After 4.5km, another track joins from the east: continue south over a stile, through a treeless plantation and over another stile to the end of the track. Cross the Allt Sloc na Creadha here, and follow the south bank of a small burn and waterfall east over a steep knoll. From this point, climb easier grassy slopes to the summit of Meall Buidhe (GR498499) (4h). Continue southwards along the top of this fine ridge, follow a series of cairns east over Meall a'Phuill and drop down to a boggy bealach. Ascend a vague ridge ENE to the summit of Cam Chreag and its numerous rocky knolls (GR536492) (5h40). Follow a track north over the ridge and, where it starts to disappear into the mire,

◄ At the west end of Loch Rannoch

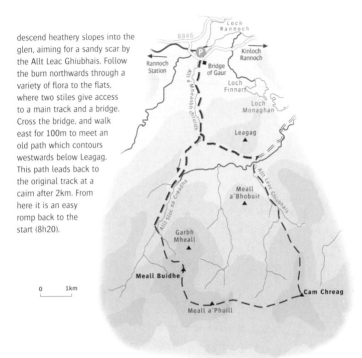

descend heathery slopes into the glen, aiming for a sandy scar by the Allt Leac Ghiubhais. Follow the burn northwards through a variety of flora to the flats, where two stiles give access to a main track and a bridge. Cross the bridge, and walk east for 100m to meet an old path which contours westwards below Leagag. This path leads back to the original track at a cairn after 2km. From here it is an easy romp back to the start (8h20).

Rannoch Barracks

The land of the Robertsons of Struan once stretched from Rannoch Moor to Perth. The Robertsons' support for the Jacobite Rebellion led the Hanoverian government to station soldiers at the head of Loch Rannoch, and barracks were built there in the 1750s. The estate was restored in 1784 and the family took over the barracks. During government occupation, plans to build a military road between Kinloch Rannoch and Glencoe were drawn up but construction progressed just a few miles beyond the loch after Rannoch Moor proved too difficult to drain.

This section covers a large fertile region close to Scotland's densely populated central belt.

The area straddles the Highland Boundary Fault, one of three great faultlines across the country. Land that was once as high as the Himalayas has been eroded into rounded peaks and glens, with only a few crags and defined ridges to break the uniformity of the terrain.

These hills are mostly unforested, with large tracts of farmland or bog, and are perhaps closer in form to Strathspey than to the rest of the Southern Highlands.

Among the walks in this section are three routes between Crieff and Loch Tay, and two circuits between the River Earn and Callander: highlights include Ben Chonzie and a long trek over the chiselled ridges of Ben Vorlich and Stùc a'Chroin. South of the faultline, there is an historic route in the Ochils and a circuit of the Lomond Hills.

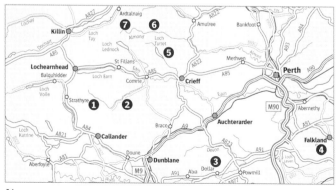

Kinross to Callander

The Ben Vorlich Arena

Ben Vorlich ⓜ (985m),
Stùc a´Chroin ⓜ (975m)

Walk time 7h40 Height gain 1300m
Distance 18km OS Map Landranger 57

**This route follows two spectacular spurs
to make an unusual horseshoe of the
peaks of Ben Vorlich and Stùc a´Chroin.**

Start 3km north of Callander at the end
of the public road, where the track divides
for Drumardoch and Braeleny Farms
(GR636107). (Parking is limited here, and it
would be better to leave cars in Callander.)
Head north on the track for 2km past
Braeleny, and cross the river to reach a farm
building and then a croft at Arivurichardich.
Keeping the croft to your right, follow a

path past enclosure walls to reach a
gateway. Beyond the gateway, climb
alongside the wall to reach a traversing
path which gains gradual height towards a
bealach at Meall na h-Iolaire. After crossing
a fence, the footpath rises through boggy
ground towards the southeast ridge of Stùc
a´Chroin. Instead of ascending this ridge,
head due north through the bealach (the
path is marked on the OS map, although
there is little trace on the ground) and
then descend into Gleann an Dubh Choirein
to reach the south ridge of Ben Vorlich.
Climb this long grassy ridge along its apex
to reach the double summit (GR629189)
(4h40). Descend on the southwest side by a
good path and fencing to Bealach an Dubh

◀ Stùc a'Chroin and Ben Vorlich

Choirein. The northeast ridge of Stùc a'Chroin looms above. Follow the fenceposts up to a large boulder field below the crags. A faint path makes a traverse around the south side of the crags at the level of the lowest boulders to reach a grassy gully. Follow the gully steeply to emerge just north of the summit (GR617175) (5h40). Descend southeast: after a steep start the terrain is easy going for 2km. The ridge then drops sharply to reach the bealach of Meall na h-Iolaire. From here, descend the path south to Arivurichardich and take the original track to the start point (7h40).

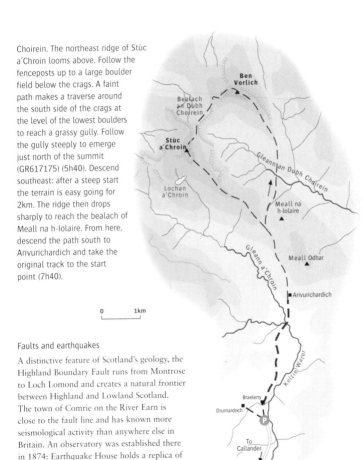

Faults and earthquakes

A distinctive feature of Scotland's geology, the Highland Boundary Fault runs from Montrose to Loch Lomond and creates a natural frontier between Highland and Lowland Scotland. The town of Comrie on the River Earn is close to the fault line and has known more seismological activity than anywhere else in Britain. An observatory was established there in 1874: Earthquake House holds a replica of the town's first seismometer.

27

Rolling Hills of Glen Artney

Am Beannan (574m), **Uamh Bheag** (664m)

Walk time 4h   Height gain 600m
Distance 11km   OS Map Landranger 57

A varied walk along the lush Glen Artney and across open moorland.

Start at the large car park by the church, 7km southwest of Dalginross (GR711161). Walk west along the road for 1.5km towards a bridge over the Water of Ruchill. Just before the bridge, pass through a gate on the left side of the road to walk upstream towards the fine spur of Am Beannan. After a while the undergrowth makes the journey more difficult, but follow the river until you reach a fence and the Allt Ollach. Accompany this burn uphill to a gate: this leads to an old bridge which will take you into open country. Continue south over easier terrain to tackle the steep but rounded buttress of Am Beannan, with its views over to Ben Vorlich. From the flat top of this hill, follow the ridge over bog: new fencing leads to Meall Clachach and Uamh Bheag. The west summit of this rounded hill is slightly higher, but the trig point is to the east (GR696117) (2h40). To descend, leave the fence and follow the northeast ridge over dips and bumps. Drop steeply to reach flat, ditched ground and the start of many small moraines. Continue northwards, rising slightly to join the Allt Môr flowing north. Follow the burn until you reach a sheep pen, then drop down to Findhu Glen, cross a bridge and go through a set of gates to reach a good track. Continue northwards to meet the road at a white gate. The start point is just a few hundred metres west (4h).

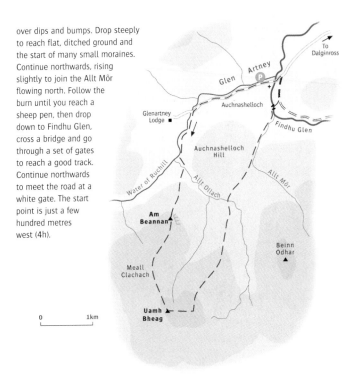

Glen Artney and Sir Walter

Glen Artney was made familiar to Victorian readers by Sir Walter Scott who featured it in two of his works. 'The Lady of the Lake' features a stag that 'deep his midnight lair had made / In lone Glenartney's hazel shade', and *A Legend of Montrose* recounts the royal forester brutally murdered while hunting deer for James VI's wedding feast. This incident had repercussions for the MacGregor clan, whose name was soon after outlawed.

◄ The bridge over the Allt Ollach

Castle Campbell and the King's Seat

King's Seat Hill (648m), **Tarmangie Hill** (645m), **Whitewisp Hill** (643m)

Walk time 4h20 Height gain 700m
Distance 11km OS Map Landranger 58

A walk in the flat-topped Ochils above Castle Campbell and the Burn of Sorrow.

Start from the information board at the Hillfoots Road car park in Dollar (GR964985). Walk north along Castle Road, and take the path on the left just after the old pumping station. This winds through trees and down to the glen. Cross at the wooden bridge, and climb switchbacks until you are above the glen. The path continues past the golf course until the castle comes into view (20 min). Here, a stile on the left leads to open country. Head west up steepening slopes to the flat top of Bank Hill and the large cairn overlooking the Forth Valley. From here the route ascends the vague southeast ridge of King's Seat Hill, passing many old watercourses and interesting mountain features before making the long climb to the summit (GR933999) (2h). Descend the steep north ridge to a secluded spot where three tributaries of the Burn of Sorrow meet.

Climb northeast up Tarmangie Hill, and then follow the wall and fence east to Whitewisp Hill. Descend the southern flank of the mountain to Saddle Hill, and then drop down over steeper slopes. At the bottom, a path contours above the Burn of Sorrow to reach the castle. Head down to the ravine on the castle's western side, cross the bridge and rejoin the original path back to Dollar (4h20).

Castle Campbell

Between the Burns of Sorrow and Care, the ruined early 15th-century Castle Campbell commands a broad view across the Forth Valley. First known as Castle Gloom, it was renamed under the ownership of the first Earl of Argyll, Colin Campbell, in 1490 and became the main Lowland residence for the family. *Glomhas* means 'horrible chasm' in Gaelic but the names of the two burns, and possibly the town of Dollar, have a more romantic origin. The daughter of a Scots king lived in the castle after being parted from her true love and is said to have named the two burns to reflect her unhappy situation. Dollar may have its roots in the word *douleur*, the French for pain.

◄ Castle Campbell from Dollar Glen

The Lomond Hills

West Lomond (522m), **Bishop Hill** (460m)

Walk time 4h40 Height gain 400m
Distance 14km OS Map Landranger 58

**An intricate route over moor and
farmland on good paths and without too
much ascent.**

Start at the car park and picnic site at
Craigmead (GR227063). Follow the signs to
West Lomond, which lead you out to the
north of the trees and onto the open hill.
From here, a path takes you westwards
between two low walls. The terrain rises
gently until the final steep incline to the
summit of West Lomond (GR197067)
(1h20). Descend by a path on the
southwest side until you reach a dry-stone
dyke with a stile. Cross the stile, and follow
the path south to a flat section by eroded
mounds. A tiny path starts from a boulder
and heads down through the heather before
fading out. Continue south to Glen Vale.
From here, a track climbs south beside a
wall. Follow this for 400m to a gateway on
the right. Pass through the gateway and
head west along a vague path through a
beautiful spot guarded by old pine. Climb
south to find the main path which follows
the ridge to Bishop Hill (GR185044) (2h40).
From the summit, rejoin the path and follow
it for just 50m to a gate. Beyond, take the
grassy track ESE. This leads through another

gate, bearing easily down to a forest and re-emerging in the fields of West Feal Farm. From here, take the track eastwards to West Balgothrie (GR226033), and then follow signs for Craigmead. This starts as a track which bypasses a reservoir, and then continues through a clearing in the forest.

Continue to follow the signposts as the route becomes a path and skirts first around Balgothrie Farm and then Ballo Reservoir to reach a boathouse. At this point, head northeast, pass through a gate by trees and climb steeply to the road. This leaves only 1km back to the start (4h40).

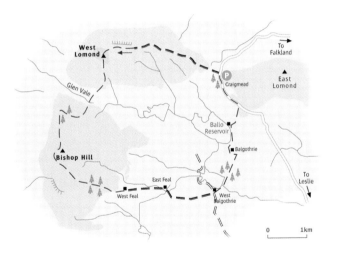

The Lomond Hills and Ben Lomond

The connection between the Lomond Hills that rise above Loch Leven in Fife and Ben Lomond, which is a source of the River Leven, in the west comes from the pre-Gaelic word for beacon, *llumon*. Both 'Lomond' and 'Leven' are derived from this root. The Lomonds were significant beacon hills in ancient times: on a clear day Ben Lomond can be seen from Glasgow and further south, and the Lomond Hills from Dundee and Edinburgh. Both can be seen from Stirling Castle.

◀ West Lomond from Burnside

33

Ben Chonzie and Loch Turret

Càrn Chòis (786m), **Ben Chonzie** ⓜ(931m)

Walk time 6h Height gain 700m
Distance 17km OS Map Landranger 52

A route that takes in a gentle peak and descends through the glacial features of the upper Glen Turret.

Start from the end of the Scottish Hydro-Electric road which leads from Glenturret Distillery to the dam (GR821265). Walk to the top of the dam on the west side and bear northwest along a track above the water. Where the track ends, follow a natural line that rises westwards. Further up, cross a fence by a rusty gate and head for the ridge to follow a fence to the rocky summit of Càrn Chòis (GR792278) (2h). Descend northwest over scree, across undulating moorland to Meall na Séide, and then through rabbit country to ascend the broad and gentle southern flanks of Ben Chonzie. Swing northeast to follow the main ridge, where a series of narrow cairns mark the route to the summit (GR773308) (4h). Descend northeast by fenceposts, steeply at first, then levelling out and dropping once again. At a bealach before Biorach a'Mheannain, descend steeply

southeast into the corrie. This is less difficult than it looks, and you soon reach Lochan Uaine which is half-covered by marsh. Follow a good earthy track down the glen from here, watching for the excellent examples of glacial moraines on the way. At a fork, take the low road which leads you back to the start (6h).

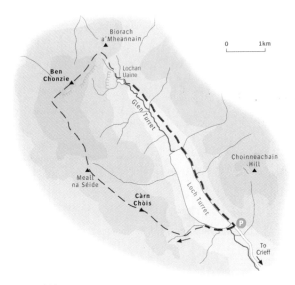

Glenturret Whisky

The waters that run from Ben Chonzie to Loch Turret are the chief ingredient for the whisky made at Glenturret, the oldest working distillery in Scotland. Although the buildings were established in 1775, illicit distilling in bothies was recorded as early as 1717. One of the first distilleries to open its doors to the public, Glenturret now receives more than 250,000 visitors every year. The whitewashed buildings were also once home to Towser, the famous World Mousing Champion cat who lived in the stillhouse for 24 years and claimed the lives of 28,899 mice.

◀ Muthill with the Crieff hills beyond

Above Glen Almond

Beinn na Gainimh (730m), **Geal Charn** (686m), **Meall Reamhar** (667m)

Walk time 6h Height gain 600m
Distance 17km OS Map Landranger 52

A peaceful walk through the wide glen of the River Almond and across the tops: a pleasure for lovers of moorland.

Start at the parking place on the A822 at Newton Bridge (GR889314). Take the track on the north side of the bridge, and follow the River Almond upstream for about 4km. Just after a bridge over a burn, watch for a

stony track which winds north up the hillside. This climbs steeply at first but, when it eases off and takes you away from the ridge after 1km, leave the track and head straight up to the obelisk at the top of the ridge (GR843331) (2h40). Continue northwest over undulating ground, making the gradual climb to the top of the moor: few features indicate Sròn Bealaidh or Beinn na Gainimh beyond. Drop north into a hollow and pick up fenceposts which now lead southeast: first over a pronounced and rocky hump, and then across 2km of bog to

the rounded top of Geal Charn. Walk eastwards to reach a low wall, which should be followed until you can contour southeast to begin your climb to the summit and trig point of Meall Reamhar. Descend ENE for about 500m, then bear southeast to find a burn which drops steeply to the east. Follow this down to meadow below. Head for a small bridge where a gate lets you onto the road and back to the start (6h).

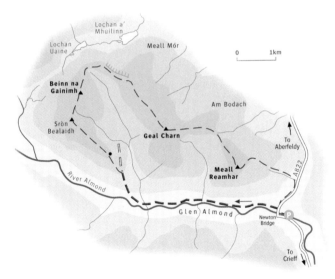

Bogs galore

Bog is a Gaelic word which denotes the soft ground covering much of Scotland. Bogs are waterlogged, acidic and low in nutrients, and support an unusual ecosystem. Sphagnum (or bog moss) is a simple rootless plant that sponges up nutrients: it is too heavy with water to grow vertically but spreads out as a mat. When old plants die, they are compressed to form a peaty underlayer which accumulates by about 1mm per year. It may come as no surprise that Scotland has more than one million hectares of bog.

◄ Sròn Bealaidh above Glen Almond

Creagan na Beinne and Loch Tay

Creagan na Beinne ⒸG (888m)

Walk time 6h Height gain 800m
Distance 17km OS Map Landranger 51 or 52

A varied walk along wide glens and over gently rolling hills at the watershed between Loch Tay and Glen Almond.

Start from the telephone box in the small village of Milton (GR702393). (Park in Milton.) Follow the minor road signposted for Glen Almond, heading southeast past a few houses to the large farm at Claggan. Go through the farm, and take the left fork at a junction: this leads to the river which is crossed by a wooden bridge. After the bridge, leave the track and walk behind an old ruin to ascend grassy slopes, keeping a burn to the left and a plantation to the right. Pass through a gate and climb broad slopes east to a fence. Follow this to the apex of the ridge, pass through another gate, and then continue to climb gently to the summit of Creagan na Beinne (GR744368) (3h). Descend a vague ridge due south and locate a grassy track which leads steeply down to the refurbished croft at Dunan. [Escape: a track leads northwards directly back to the start.] Follow a track southwest, behind the cottage and level with a burn, to reach a footbridge after 300m. From here, walk upstream by a burn that flows from the northwest. This is tougher going but comes to a fence and gate at a bealach after 2km, with a new track just beyond. Follow this down the glen for about 2.5km to an intersection. Take the track on the left northwards over the burn and through a gate: it starts to

deteriorate as it contours around the ridge. Watch for a narrow gate in a deer fence on the right about 1km after the fork. Pass through this to find an old path in a runnel. This zigzags its way down through lush flora to the minor road near the start (6h).

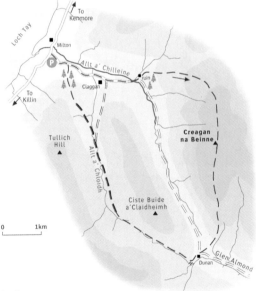

The mighty Tay

The River Tay can claim to be the greatest river in Britain as, by the time it reaches the North Sea, it has discharged a volume of water larger than that of the Thames and Severn basins combined. In the 70 miles from its natural reservoir of Loch Tay to the coast, the river winds through some of the finest scenery in central Scotland and is crossed by 20 bridges, the first of which is at Kenmore. Each year on 15 January the Taymouth Estate hosts the opening ceremony of the salmon fishing season at the Kenmore Hotel, the oldest tavern in Scotland.

◀ Creagan na Beinne across Loch Tay

A spectacular mix of narrow lochs, peninsulas and high peaks makes the Arrochar Alps a place for adventure.

The hills feel almost alpine with steep crags, defined ridges and high meadows, but the name originates from the early climbers, particularly those from Glasgow, who came here to train for higher pursuits in the Alps or Greater Ranges.

The Cobbler is a year-round favourite with climbers, while the deep lochs of Lomond, Long, Goil, Fyne and Eck are known for sailing and other watersports. Private boats offer the best transport to some remoter spots.

Lochs feature in all of the routes in this section. Beinn Bhuidhe is approached from Loch Fyne, close to Inveraray. Loch Goil is the starting point for a circuit high above Carrick Castle. Three of the routes, including The Cobbler, begin from the heart of the Arrochar Alps on the northern shore of Loch Long. A further three walks overlook Loch Lomond: Ben Vorlich is reached from Ardlui on the western shore; a half-day route around Glen Finlas starts south of Luss; and

Ben Lomond is accessed from Rowardennan. Strictly speaking, Ben Lomond is not part of the Arrochar Alps, but its character is more suited to this area than to the Trossachs.

All of the hills in this section, with the exception of Beinn Bhuidhe, are part of the Loch Lomond and The Trossachs National Park.

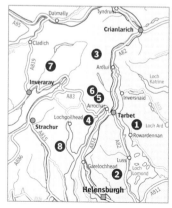

The Arrochar Alps

Ben Lomond

Ben Lomond ⓜ (974m)

Walk time 5h Height gain 1000m
Distance 12km OS Map Landranger 56

Ben Lomond is perhaps the Southern Highlands' most popular peak, with views over Loch Lomond and its many islands.

Start at the large forest car park just beyond the hotel at Rowardennan (GR360984). A marked trail leads from the car park, and begins to climb eastwards through trees. After 1.5km, the path emerges onto open hill by a gate and continues to climb, rising more steeply by a burn and then levelling out. (Restoration work has much improved this path, once 25m wide in places.) Continue northwards along the wide ridge of Sron Aonaich, and then follow a series of switchbacks which lead to the summit ridge. Taken on the south side to avoid cliffs, this leads to the summit and trig point (GR367028) (3h20). Descend steeply to the northwest along

a well-defined and rocky ridge with a good path until you reach a flat boggy area with stepping stones. Walk southwest over undulating ground for a short distance and then drop south along the Ptarmigan ridge, still following a good path which zigzags easily. Lower down, pass through a gate and keep lochside while descending through bracken. Another gate brings you out to the private road, and from here it is a short walk south to the start (5h).

Islands of Loch Lomond

At 37km long and 8km across at its widest, Loch Lomond is the largest freshwater loch in Scotland. There are more than 30 islands located mostly at the south end, many of them home to unusual wildlife. Wallabies were introduced to Inchconnachan and fallow deer can sometimes be seen swimming across the water. The islands also have their place in history. In the 14th century, Inchlonaig was planted with yew trees to supply the bows that were used at the Battle of Bannockburn. Many of the islands were also used to distil illicit whisky until HM Customs & Excise clamped down on the practice in the mid-19th century.

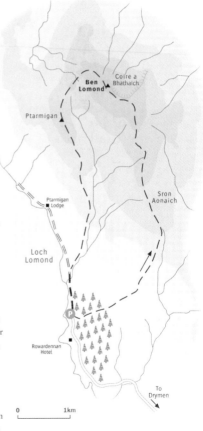

◄ Ben Lomond from Milton, near Aberfoyle

43

Around Glen Finlas

Creag an Leinibh (657m), **Unnamed** (693m), **Balcnock** (638m)

Walk time 5h20 Height gain 700m
Distance 15km OS Map Landranger 56

This moorland route follows the natural watershed around Glen Finlas and overlooks Loch Lomond.

Start at the intersection between the A82 and the A817, 4km south of Luss (GR353883). Walk up the steep private road marked for Shemore and Shegarton. Turn left at the farm at Shemore and cross several cattle grids, heading towards the terraced buildings below the dam. Shortly before the buildings, take the steep gravel track on the right which leads through trees to the top of the dam. From here, a good path gains height above the water and then fades. Continue northwest over boggy ground at the same level for another 1km until you reach a steep tree-lined ravine. Cross the burn to climb due north up grassy slopes for some distance. Higher up, these relent and peat hags begin to appear. Join the ridge proper to follow an old fence over the tops, and continue northwest to Creag an Leinibh (GR311919). The ridge wheels around to the WSW with views of Luss Water to the north. Climb steeply to a high point (3h20). Continue to follow the fenceposts southeast, and then turn SSW at a large cairn to reach Balcnock. Descend the southeast ridge. This becomes increasingly wet underfoot, culminating in proper bog 2km further on at Craperoch

(GR321888). At this point, the fence is joined by another from the south. Climb over the small mound on the ridge and bear east, descending easy grassy slopes towards the foot of Loch Finlas. On reaching the water, pass over a fence by the iron stile, cross the dam and find the original track back to the start (5h20).

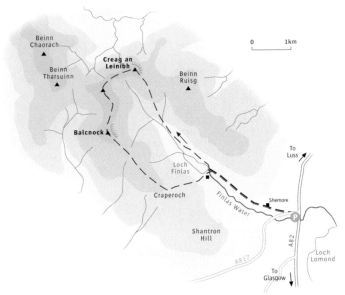

Great leaps

In the winter of 1603, after a brief battle with the MacGregors of Glenfruin, McLintock, a Colquhoun of Luss, became separated from the rest of his clan. With MacGregors giving chase, he escaped over Shantron Hill and leapt the 7m chasm of Finlas Water to safety (now beneath the A817 roadbridge). This is just one of a number of leaps in the Southern Highlands, including the 5.5m Soldier's Leap at Killiecrankie and MacGregor's Leap in Glen Lyon, a reconstruction of which led to the death of an athlete in 1890. The current world long jump record stands at just over 8.9m.

◄ *Maid of the Loch* at Balloch with the Luss Hills beyond

Ben Vorlich over Loch Lomond

Ben Vorlich ⓜ (943m), Little Hills (808m)

Walk time 4h40 Height gain 1000m
Distance 11km OS Map Landranger 56

A popular peak by Britain's largest freshwater loch. There are great views into the Arrochar Alps from the summit and an entertaining descent.

Start from the A82 at Ardlui (GR316155). Walk south along the road for 300m beyond the railway station, passing a tunnel for a small track to a house on the right. Go through the next pass under the railway. From here, take a path which rises gently south over bracken-covered slopes. The path accompanies a burn for a short distance, passes through a gate and reaches a dam and water catchment pipes. Continue to climb before reaching the flatter, boggy ground below Coire Creagach. Now heading northwest, climb to the ridgeline shared with Stob nan Coinnich Bhacain. Follow the ridge southwest and then south, avoiding small buttresses, to reach the summit plateau of Ben Vorlich. This is quite a long section with numerous cairns, but it is worth visiting the south end for the views down Loch Lomond (GR295124) (3h20). Descend northeast towards a small lochan and then continue to drop east through complex terrain, avoiding a series of broken cliffs, to reach a bealach. Climb steeply to

◀ Looking south along Loch Lomond

the top of Little Hills, keeping to the north side, then drop again and climb to another top. Descend the ridge northeast through complex troughs and folds for 2km. The ridge ends in a steeper section: keep to the north side to arrive at a flat grassy area and a fence with a stile. Cross the stile and descend northeast, keeping between the burn and a fenced field. Pass through a gate and turn left along a track. This ends after about 150m at a burn hidden in the trees. Cross this, and climb over a wooden gate. Head north to meet the original path. Pass under the railway and continue north up the road to finish (4h40).

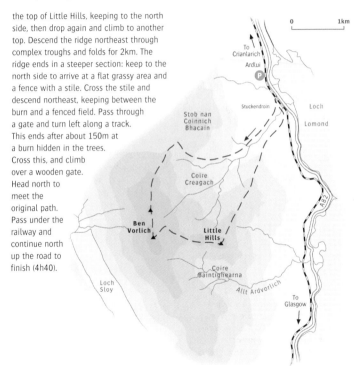

The bonnie, bonnie banks

The song 'The Bonnie Banks o'Loch Lomond' was composed by Donald MacDonell of Keppoch in Carlisle jail in the aftermath of the Jacobite defeat at Culloden. English justice was unpredictable and while some prisoners were freed and allowed to walk home on the 'low road', MacDonell was sure he was heading for the gallows and the 'high road'. Sadly, he was correct.

The Brack

The Brack ◐ (787m)

Walk time 4h40 Height gain 800m
Distance 12km OS Map Landranger 56

A steep initial climb to the top of a rocky peak with a descent along good forestry tracks.

Start from the Forestry Commission Information Centre 1km north of Ardgartan caravan site (GR269037). Walk over the bridge, and take the track on the left signposted for The Brack. Rise gently through plantations for 2km to reach a fork. Take the right fork, and watch for a signposted path after about 100m. This path follows a burn as it rises steeply south beneath the formidable cliffs of The Brack. Climb to a bealach shared with Cruach Fhiarach, and then follow the vague east ridge of The Brack to its summit (GR245030) (2h20). To descend, follow the southwest ridge, taking care to avoid bands of cliffs in the upper section. Lower down, the ridge flattens out except for one last knoll which leads to a bealach shared with Cnoc Coinnich. Pass through a gate and descend east by a fence to the forest. Cross a stile to reach a forest path, and follow this steeply down by a burn. A bridge crosses the burn by newly harvested trees. Soon after, the path becomes a track and leads down to Coilessan Glen. After 2km, follow a tarmac road north: this leads back to the information centre (4h40).

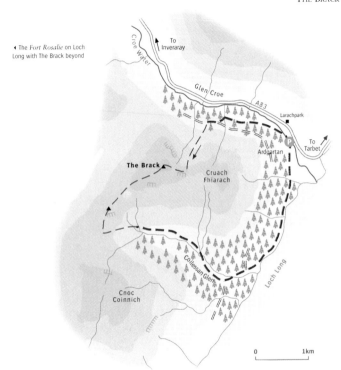

◄ The *Fort Rosalie* on Loch Long with The Brack beyond

The Vikings in Arrochar

In 1263, King Haakon of Norway launched an invasion to re-assert his control over Kintyre and the Western Isles in response to Alexander III's attempt to buy back the Hebrides. With a fleet of up to 200 longships, Haakon's forces sailed south. Fifty galleys headed up Loch Long and were hauled over the isthmus to Tarbet before resuming sail and plundering the settlements around Loch Lomond. They continued down the River Leven to the Firth of Clyde where they rejoined Haakon's forces for the shambolic Battle of Largs. An equinoctial gale scattered the Viking fleet, making a complete landing impossible, and Alexander's forces were able to repel the attack with far fewer men. King Haakon died later that year in Orkney, and his lands finally passed back to Scotland with the Treaty of Perth in 1266.

The Cobbler and his wife

Ben Arthur (The Cobbler) Ⓖ (884m),
Beinn Narnain Ⓜ (926m)

Walk time 5h Height gain 1200m
Distance 10km OS Map Landranger 56

**Great views and exciting terrain make
The Cobbler a favourite with many
walkers. The paths are good and
scrambling is optional.**

Start from the lochside car park just south
of the turning for Succoth (GR294048).
Cross the road, walk south and take the
path on the right after 30m. This climbs
through a plantation, and then crosses a
track before zigzagging steeply on the north
bank of the Allt a'Bhalachain to reach a
small dam. Continue more easily upstream
and, after passing the Narnain Boulders,
cross the burn to head west towards The
Cobbler. Leave the path soon after to bear
south across boggy ground into the main
amphitheatre, and then aim for the
southeast ridge of The Cobbler. Thread your
way through boulders, then skirt along the
south side of the ridge under large cliffs.
There are three summits to this peak. The
large cioch on the ridge (optional) calls for
some tricky scrambling. The central summit
is easier, but the final few metres (optional)
are also exposed. The main north summit,
which is reached from a bealach, involves
easy climbing over worn slabs. Care should

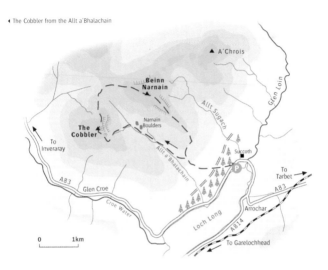

◄ The Cobbler from the Allt a'Bhalachain

be taken as there are cliffs all around (GR262060) (3h). From the main summit, return to the bealach and make the steep descent on the west side of the north ridge by a good path. This brings you to a bealach shared with Beinn Narnain. Bear northeast on the path, which now starts to climb up the west ridge to finally reach the summit plateau (GR272066) (4h). Descend the east ridge by another path. Very soon this steepens: descend a rocky gully to find a series of switchbacks on the south side of the ridge which lead down to easier terrain. Drop down on the east side of the ridge to reach a good path by the foot of the spur. This contours west to the dam across the Allt a'Bhalachain. Follow the path back to the road (5h).

The Cobbler Club

The climbing routes of the Arrochar Alps are an important part of Scottish mountaineering history. The Cobbler Club was founded in 1866 by George Ramsay, an accomplished climber from Glasgow University. In the 1930s, changes in work and society as well as better transport from Glasgow led to another, more populist wave of interest in mountaineering. The area is still very popular for summer and winter climbing.

this becomes more defined and is easily
followed to the top (GR243079). Descend
eastwards over terraced ground to a
bealach. From here, climb steeply northeast
past numerous small crags on the east side
of Beinn Ime to the stone shelter at the
summit (GR255084) (3h). Descend on the
north side to Glas Bhealach. Climb north to
the top of Beinn Chorranach for the best
view of the meandering Allt Coiregrogain,
and then return to the bealach. Drop
eastwards to meet a small burn: this leads
to a boggy bealach at Lag Uaine, an
entertaining descent which is never too
steep. Follow a vague ridge eastwards,
avoiding small crags, and climb to the
summit of Ben Vane (GR278098) (4h40).
Descend northwest along the ridge to a flat,

boggy area and a small lochan. Continue northwards over knolls and past fine quartz veins to the top of Beinn Dubh. Drop directly on the west side, following the easiest terrain: grassy slopes eventually lead to the glen and a track. Go through the deer fence by a gate at the top end of the track, and head along the burn to pass Abyssinia. Cross the Kinglas Water to reach the track along the glen. Follow this southwest for 3km back to the start point (7h).

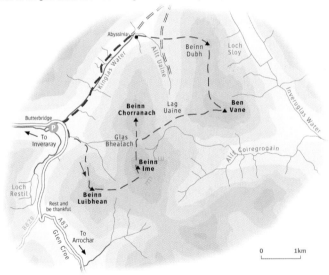

Abyssinia

Abyssinia, the house and former bothy in Glen Kinglas, got its unlikely name from Iain Mór (Big John), a local man who served with the British Army in Africa in the late 19th century. An expeditionary force led by Sir Robert Napier deposed the Abyssinian king after the British consul, Captain Charles Duncan Cameron, had been imprisoned. Big John played his part in the episode and liked to reminisce about his soldiering so much that the name Abyssinia became attached to his home.

◀ Looking west from Ben Vane into Argyll

Glen Shira to Beinn Bhuidhe

Beinn Chas (680m),
Beinn Bhuidhe Ⓜ (948m)

Walk time 4h40 Height gain 1000m
Approach and return 2h bike or 5h walk
Distance 12km + 20km approach and return
OS Map Landranger 56

**Beinn Bhuidhe is an isolated peak
wedged between Glen Shira and Glen
Fyne. The approach along forestry roads
is long, and a mountain bike is advised.**

Start from the north end of Loch Shira, at
the parking area before the entrance to the
Argyll Estate (GR112103). Take the private
tarmac road north past Dubh Loch and

along Glen Shira for about 5km. Just
beyond Elrigmhor, there is a gate and stile:
proceed beyond into Forestry Commission
land where the road begins to climb. It
soon turns eastwards, with several
switchbacks as it gains height. Continue for
3km to a bridge over the Brannie Burn.
Instead of crossing, keep to the south of
the burn to reach a set of pylons and a
large pipeline (GR173161). Bikes are best
left here: walk times begin from this point.
Pass under the pipeline and leave the track
to climb southwards through a break in the
forest, keeping to the left of the pylons
(vague path). At the top of the plantation,

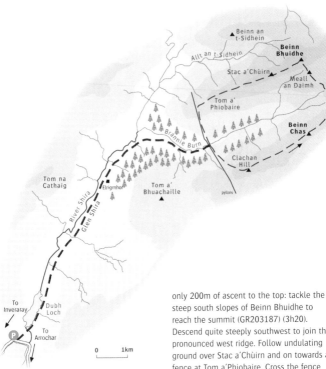

only 200m of ascent to the top: tackle the steep south slopes of Beinn Bhuidhe to reach the summit (GR203187) (3h20). Descend quite steeply southwest to join the pronounced west ridge. Follow undulating ground over Stac a'Chùirn and on towards a fence at Tom a'Phiobaire. Cross the fence on the north side of the ridge where a post will help. Shortly after, a southwesterly descent off the ridge should bring you to the line of pylons. Follow these south through the forest break by a boggy track, and then cross the river at a weir (4h40). Follow the Brannie Burn and then the River Shira back to the start.

cross a fence at a gateway on the right. Climb east over hillocks and dips to the top of Clachan Hill. Walk ENE along the top of the undulating ridge and over Beinn Chas, then traverse northwards to a wide bealach. From here, climb northwest to the top of Meall an Daimh, a grassy knoll. This leaves

◀ Beinn Bhuidhe from Clachan Hill

Tour of Carrick Castle

Creachan Mór (657m), **Cruach a'Bhuic** (635m), **Sgurr a'Choinnich** (661m)

Walk time 5h20 Height gain 800m
Distance 14km OS Map Landranger 56

The austere tower house of Carrick Castle is the starting point for a route that rises high above Lochs Long and Goil.

Start from Carrick Castle (GR195943). Walk south along the road, past the public toilets and over a humpback bridge. Take the track on the right just after the burn, and follow it up to the edge of a fenced plantation and a gate. Do not enter the forest, but follow vague tracks that climb steeply southwards alongside the trees to a fence. Go through a gap in the fence and continue to climb, passing through a gate higher up. Where the forest ends, continue to ascend grassy slopes to the top of Cruach an Draghair. From here, head west over knolls and hollows to join the Allt Reinain. Follow this upstream towards a series of buttresses to the south: these constitute the summit of Creachan Mór and provide an ideal lookout across to Faslane (GR187916) (2h20). Follow the fenceline northwest over the undulating ridge. Pass through a gate and aim for the short but steep Cruach a'Bhuic. The ridge continues to climb northwards to Sgurr a'Choinnich and the compact set of crags at its two tops (GR159956) (4h). Drop down NNE for 1.5km to reach Cnoc na Tricriche. This gives access to a fine ridge which descends southeast

with occasional steep grassy drops, all of which can be avoided. Towards the end of the ridge, keep to the north side to reach a track above Cuilimuich. This leads down to the road: it is a short walk along the loch to the castle (5h20).

Carrick Castle and Argyll's Rising

Dating from the 15th century, Carrick Castle on Loch Goil is surrounded by water on three sides. Before its destruction, it was used as a hunting lodge, document safe and prison. The Castle was razed in 1685 in retribution for Argyll's Rising, a doomed enterprise led by Archibald Campbell, 9th Earl of Argyll, and the Duke of Monmouth. Their aim was to remove James VII, the new king, but support never materialised and Archibald was captured and lost his head in Edinburgh.

◀ Loch Goil from Carrick Castle

First popularised by Sir Walter Scott's poem, 'The Lady of the Lake', 1810, and novel *Rob Roy*, 1817, the rugged Trossachs are still a favourite with walkers, mountain bikers and day-trippers.

These hills, with their forested peaks and deep lochs, are part of the Loch Lomond and The Trossachs National Park. Lochearnhead and Glen Ogle mark the northern boundary of the Park.

Further north into the Mamlorn Hills, the peaks are higher, wilder and less forested. The whole area is rich in legend and folklore, much of it to do with feuding clans and cattle raiding. This is also Rob Roy country, and the outlaw's image and name can be found on everything from shortbread tins and tea towels to guesthouses and pubs.

This section features two walks in the Trossachs, including an ascent of Ben Ledi, and two more demanding and less frequented circuits that start at Balquhidder and Loch Voil. Four routes take in the peaks of Mamlorn, near Killin: one reached from the wide strath of Glen Dochart and three from the tranquil Glen Lochay.

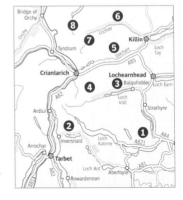

The Trossachs to the Mamlorn Hills

Ben Ledi of the Trossachs

Ben Ledi ❺ (879m),
Ardnandave Hill (722m)

Walk time 5h Height gain 800m
Distance 12km OS Map Landranger 57

A popular route with rewarding views over the forested peaks and glens of the Trossachs.

Start at the iron bridge at the south end of Loch Lubnaig, signposted for Strathyre Forest Cabins (GR587093). A path leads from the west side of the bridge into forest, climbing quickly through the trees to a track. Cross the track to find another path, this time marked with green posts. This leads through a harvested plantation and across the occasional boardwalk to a burn. Follow the path upstream, keeping to the south bank of the burn and aiming for a band of cliffs. After a while, it crosses the burn and passes southwards under the bluffs to meet the southeast ridge of Ben Ledi and a line of posts. Bear northwest to follow the ridge to the summit (GR563098) (2h20). Descend the north ridge, following the old fence down to the first small bealach and a cairn. [Escape: descend on the eastern side to join a well-defined but eroded path which leads down to the forestry tracks.] Continue north over undulating ground, following the fenceline for about 300m beyond the high point of the ridge. Descend northeast towards Ardnandave Hill: this is complex terrain with many folds and dips. Cross a double fence and continue east to the summit, climbing steeply to finish (GR567125) (3h40). Descend SSE over similar ground.

◄ Ben Ledi from Achray Forest

The south ridge becomes more defined further down. Keep to the corrie side on approaching Stank Glen, passing through an old plantation to reach a track near a burn. Turn left along the track and turn right at the first junction. After some dips and rises, watch for a small path on the left,

marked with new green posts. This descends through old forest, passing a hidden waterfall, to emerge by two parallel roads at the level of the loch. Choose the lochside road which leads south to the start point (5h).

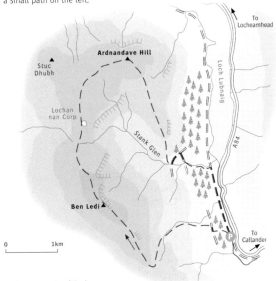

Beltane and the mountain of God

Taking its name from *Beinn le Dia*, the mountain of God, Ben Ledi has an ancient history as a place of pre-Christian worship. The Beltane festival, the Celtic new year, would have seen people gather to welcome the dawn and celebrate the coming of spring on the mountainside. Large crowds still gather on Calton Hill and Arthur's Seat in Edinburgh to celebrate the lighting of the *Bealltainn* fires.

Beinn a'Choin and Rob's Cave

Beinn a'Choin  (770m)

Walk time 5h20 Height gain 800m
Distance 13km OS Map Landranger 56

A fine peak above three lochs, with few paths and an adventurous and tricky descent. This route can be approached by private ferry across Loch Lomond from Inveruglas or on the Loch Katrine steamship from the Trossachs pier to Stronachlachar, 6km east of Inversnaid.

Start from the Inversnaid Hotel on the east bank of Loch Lomond (GR337089). Walk east up the road to the school and the old garrison, built to stop local cattle raiding and capture Rob Roy. Just after the

school, take the track north. Follow this past a house on the right and up the glen. After 1km, the track ends at a gate. Pass through the gate to climb northeast over rough ground by a burn, heading in the direction of the Bealach a'Mheim until you reach a fence. Follow this north on either side – the terrain makes for eventful climbing – to the summit of Beinn a'Choin (GR355130) (3h). To descend, follow the county boundary due west to the shores of Loch Lomond. The boundary is marked by a low wall at first, but when this disappears follow a burn down to flatter terrain. From here, keep to the north of the fences which protect the nature reserve to the southwest. Watch for another small burn which

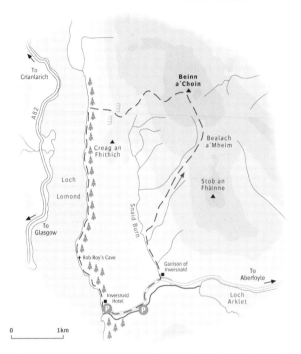

cascades through boulders and steep forest to Loch Lomond. Stay left of the burn on descent: it is easier than it looks but still provides some adventure and can be very slippery further down. From the loch shore, the West Highland Way leads easily southwards, passing Rob Roy's Cave on the return to the hotel (5h20).

The RSPB in Scotland

The Inversnaid Reserve by Loch Lomond contains several habitat types: the loch is used by migrating goldeneyes and whooper swans; the burns attract common sandpipers and dippers; the deciduous forest is home to great spotted woodpecker and various warblers; the crags are occupied by buzzards; and grouse are occasionally seen on the moorland above. The area is fenced off to prevent deer and sheep from removing sources of food, nesting materials and protective foliage.

◀ Loch Lomond and Loch Long from Beinn a'Choin

63

Rob Roy's Run

Meall an Fhiodhain (817m), **Cam Chreag** (812m), **Meall an t-Seallaidh** ● (852m)

Walk time 5h Height gain 900m
Distance 12km OS Map Landranger 51

An historic route which starts out from Rob Roy's grave. The bealach by Lochan an Eireannaich was a likely shortcut to Glen Dochart for the Highland outlaw.

Start from the churchyard containing Rob Roy's grave in Balquhidder (GR536209). Take the track on the east side of the church, and follow it for 100m into the forest. Cross the stile on the right, which is signposted for Creag an Tuirc, and follow the track northwards up Kirkton Glen until you reach a fork after about 3km. Take the right fork and turn immediately left onto a path that leads north. This rises quickly past large boulders to the Lochan an Eireannaich (GR514244) (2h). Leave the path here and climb northeast, keeping to the far north side of the crags and loosely following an old fence. Once above the cliffs, continue northeast to the apex of the ridge. Drop down on the east side and wade eastwards across boggy, undulating terrain, following a different line of fenceposts southeast to Meall an Fhiodhain and beyond to Cam Chreag. From here, it is a final gentle climb southwards to the summit of Meall an t-Seallaidh (GR542234) (4h). Descend southeast by another fence for about 1.5km to reach a wide plateau. Drop southwest, avoiding a small crag lower down. Aim for the northeast corner of the plantation, and

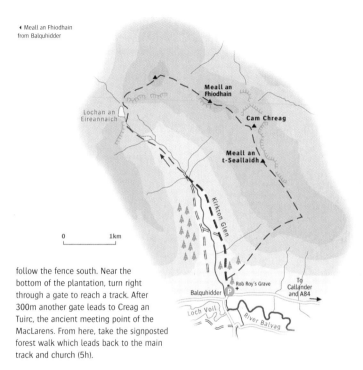

◀ Meall an Fhiodhain from Balquhidder

Meall an Fhiodhain

Cam Chreag

Meall an t-Seallaidh

Lochan an Eireannaich

Kirkton Glen

0   1km

Rob Roy's Grave

Balquhidder

To Callander and A84

Loch Voil

River Balvag

follow the fence south. Near the bottom of the plantation, turn right through a gate to reach a track. After 300m another gate leads to Creag an Tuirc, the ancient meeting point of the MacLarens. From here, take the signposted forest walk which leads back to the main track and church (5h).

The Highland hero

Rob 'Roy' MacGregor became known for his exceptional skill with a broadsword as a youth, fighting at Killiecrankie for 'Bonnie Dundee'. He prospered through his acquisitions of land and cattle until a charge of embezzlement by the Duke of Montrose in 1712 made him an outlaw with a price on his head. He nevertheless led his clan in the first Jacobite rising and, after many adventures, died in his bed while a piper played at his side. He is buried at Balquhidder Church: the inscription on his grave, *MacGregor Despite Them*, refers to an edict by James VI in 1603 which banned use of the clan name. The law was not revoked for another 172 years.

The Boulders of Cruach Ardrain

Stob Garbh (959m), **Cruach Ardrain** Ⓜ
(1046m), **Beinn Tulaichean** Ⓜ (946m)

Walk time 6h Height gain 1000m
Distance 14km
OS Maps Landranger 56, 57 and 51

**A varied circuit with some steep sections
of ascent and descent. This walk affords
fine views of the mirrored twins of Ben
More and Stob Binnein. The northeast
face of Cruach Ardrain is steep, making
this a serious route in winter.**

Start from the picnic and parking spot
beyond Loch Doine (GR445185). Walk west
along the track to Inverlochlarig where a
series of signposts lead walkers across a
bridge and alongside Inverlochlarig Burn to
join a track. Follow this track north on the
west bank of the burn. After 3km, the track

ends and the burn is followed less easily to
a wide boulder-strewn bealach. Climb
westwards from here, keeping the eastern
crags of Stob Garbh to your left. Steep
banks and small terraces make for an
entertaining ascent to the summit
(GR411222) (3h20). Descend south along a
path which weaves around low buttresses
to a bealach. The steep northeast face of
Cruach Ardrain looms ahead: take the
narrow, winding path to its double summit
(GR409212). From the west top, follow the
prominent south ridge down to a gentle

bealach and continue up easy slopes to the summit of Beinn Tulaichean (GR417196) (5h). Descend SSE along the ridge, taking care as you bypass a set of cliffs. After this, the descent is fairly straightforward. Head southeast towards the farm at Inverlochlarig to join the track back to the start (6h).

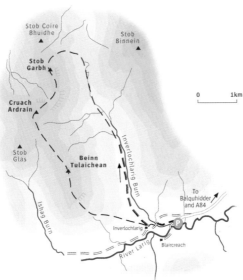

Dalradian geology

The solid geology of the Southern Highlands is composed mainly of schists from the Dalradian succession, and could be 600 million years old. The rock is thousands of feet thick and was first deposited as mud and sand in an ancient ocean, the Iapetus. The Caledonian Orogeny, a later mountain building event on the scale of the Himalayas, heated and compressed these sediments to form crystalline schists and quartzite. In 1891 Sir Archibald Geikie, then Director General of the British Survey, suggested the name Dalradian after the first kingdom of the Scots.

◄ Cruach Ardrain and Beinn Tulaichean from Stob Garbh

The Auchlyne Traverse

**Sgiath Chùil ⓜ (921m),
Meall a'Churain (918m)**

Walk time 6h20 Height gain 1000m
Distance 18km OS Map Landranger 51

**A circuit of less visited peaks between
the glens of Dochart and Lochay. A high
track makes for easy height gain.**

Start from the humpback bridge over
Auchlyne West Burn at the west end of
Auchlyne Village (GR509295). A good track
leads from the east side of the bridge and
climbs northwest, zigzagging to gain height
until it reaches a junction. Take the left
fork, which drops slightly, crosses a bridge
and then continues to rise gently. After 1km
the track fords the river (strong current after
heavy rainfall), and about 150m further on a

smaller burn appears. Leave the track and
follow the burn upstream, rising northwest
through heather and grasses until you arrive
at a flatter area before some crags. Climb
northeast, keeping the crags to your left,
and then follow the vague east ridge of
Sgiath Chrom westwards to its top. Descend
north into flat terrain, and break through a
band of crags to reach the summit of Sgiath
Chùil (GR463318) (3h40). Head due north
across undulating ground and over a
smaller top to reach the summit of Meall
a'Churain. Descend ENE, avoiding steep
cliffs on the east, to reach the flat area of
bog at Meall Eòghainn. Cross this, and
climb northeast for about 1.5km to reach a
two-headed top: the ascent involves some
uneven and often confusing terrain

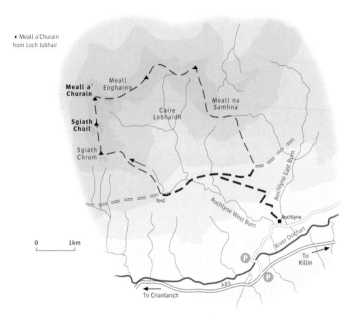

◄ Meall a'Churain
from Loch Iubhair

(GR476333). Continue over similar ground, now heading east, to another high point. Follow the prominent south ridge of this peak: this soon drops to Meall na Samhna. At a lone boulder the ridge loses definition:

drop east past a rounded hillock, contour around the edge of the ridge and then descend due south. This brings you close to the first fork in the track: take this back to Auchlyne (6h20).

The Killin MacNabs

The MacNab clan has its burial ground on the small island of Inchbuie on the Falls of Dochart, the only land left to this once influential clan. They were too often in debt or in dispute with the Breadalbane Campbells and eventually, in 1828, the 4th Earl of Breadalbane gained much of the MacNab land including Kinnell House, the clan seat, and many MacNabs emigrated. The most legendary chief was Francis, 'a prodigious consumer of whisky' who fathered more than 100 children and never married. 'MacNab's porridge cart' was said to leave Kinnell House every morning to dispense oatmeal to the bairns of the laird.

Meall Ghaordaidh via the old path

Meall Ghaordaidh (1039m)

Walk time 6h Height gain 900m
Distance 15km OS Map Landranger 51

A high peak reached from the remains of an old settlement above Glen Lochay over a mixture of good paths and rough terrain.

Start from a tarmac track which joins the road through Glen Lochay about 800m west of the power station (GR538353). (Limited parking here.) The track climbs north between trees, passes through a gate after 200m and then, still rising, swings east. Ignore an unmarked turning and continue east along the track until it turns and ends at a fenced area where visitors are clearly not welcome. Skirt around the lower side of this land to pick up an old path leading northwest: after a short while this may seem to fade out. A low, broken wall appears after about 300m: climb up alongside it to rejoin the path. This crosses several small burns by way of railway sleepers and rusty iron girders, and must once have been well-used. Follow it northwest for about 2km until you reach the remains of an old settlement at the confluence of several burns. Continue upriver, and cross the first burn after about 400m to avoid difficult terrain. Cross again to the point where the Allt Dhùin Croisg and the Allt na h-Iolaire meet (beside a large rock pool), and follow the latter burn north over the moorland between Cam Chreag and Beinn nan Oighreag. After about 2km, the burn all but disappears: head northwest to attain the ridge of Cam Chreag by two diamond-shaped crags, and follow this southwest to the top. Drop a short distance before climbing the last slopes to the summit of Meall Ghaordaidh (GR514397) (4h20). Descend by a path along the southeast ridge. Keep to the

apex as far as possible and, as you reach the glen, bear towards the north side of a fenced field to reach a track. This leads south past an old shieling to a walled field and gate. Pass through the field and two more gates to reach the road. From here, it

is 1.5km back to the start, with some good examples of pre-Christian cup-marked stones along the way (6h).

The coffin roads

The earliest paths in the Highlands were those worn by people going between settlements, peat bogs for fuel, mills and churches. Among the earliest long-distance tracks, however, were the coffin roads. As it was the custom of Highlanders to be buried alongside their forefathers, coffin-bearers often had to travel many miles. When stopping for a break the funeral party would build cairns on which they rested the coffin and these still exist, maintained by passers-by over the years. There is an ancient Gaelic curse on those who pass by such a cairn without adding a respectful stone, although these days walkers are encouraged not to do so by the Scottish Mountaineering Club.

◀ Meall Ghaordaidh and Ben Lawers from the west

Meall Glas and Glen Lochay

Beinn Cheathaich (937m),
Meall Glas ⓜ(959m)

Walk time 3h40 Height gain 800m
Approach and return 1h bike or 2h walk
Distance 9km + 8km approach and return
OS Map Landranger 51

**A short route on the south side of
the picturesque Glen Lochay. Use of
a mountain bike will reduce the overall
time taken on this circuit.**

Start at the end of the public road beyond
Kenknock in Glen Lochay (GR466365). Walk
or cycle west along the farm track, through
several gates and beyond a plantation to
the turn-off for Badour (GR432350). Leave
bikes here: walk times are given from this
point. Descend to the River Lochay and
cross by a wooden bridge. Climb southwards
to join the Allt Coire Cheathaich: higher up,
pass through a gate and follow the west
side of the leaping burn steeply upstream
until the terrain eases. Cross the water just
below some hidden ruins and head
southeast, climbing even, grassy slopes to
the vague north ridge of Beinn Cheathaich
and on to the summit (GR444327) (2h).
Descend southwest, passing slabs of folded

rock, to reach a smaller top. Drop again, and head west over undulating terrain before the short push to the summit of Meall Glas (GR432323) (2h40). Descend northwest along a ridge: this becomes more defined as you continue. After 1km descend due north to avoid steeper ground, but then resume a northwesterly bearing, circumnavigating small cliffs, to

reach a rickety bridge across the River Lochay. Just downstream, a gravel track descends from the north: follow this east past Batavaime to Badour (3h40). Peddle or walk from here to the start.

Moirlanich Longhouse

Moirlanich Longhouse is a traditional cruck frame cottage on the outskirts of Killin, now owned by the National Trust for Scotland and open to visitors. Longhouses were originally built to accommodate livestock as well as people, with a cow or two sleeping on one side of the dwelling through the winter. Built low to withstand storms and retain heat, the longhouses were usually built to conform to the old Gaelic proverb, 'East to west, the house that's best – back to the wind and face to the sun'.

◀ Looking east along Glen Lochay from the Allt Coire Cheathaich

73

Peaks of Mamlorn

Creag Mhór ⓜ (1047m),
Beinn Heasgarnich ⓜ (1078m)

Walk time 7h Height gain 1200m
Approach and return 1h20 bike or 2h40 walk
Distance 18km + 11km approach and return
OS Maps Landranger 50 and 51

A walk over two fine mountains at the head of Glens Lochay and Lyon. Use of a bike gives the best access to the start.

Start at the end of the public road beyond Kenknock in Glen Lochay (GR466365). Walk or cycle west along the farm track, through several gates, beyond a plantation and past the turn-offs for Badour and Batavaime. Just after the farm at Batavaime, the track begins to climb. Bikes should be left here: walk times start at this point. Continue up the track and go straight on at the junction, after which it begins to zigzag. After gaining about 150m in height, it joins another track. Take this second track west, and contour under Sròn nan Eun. After 1.5km, the track loses some height before meeting the Allt Cheathaich. At this point, head northwest over grass and through a gate to follow the burn past boulders and pools. Cross the burn, and aim for the buttresses of Sail Dhubh which can be breached by a grassy gully to reach a

◀ The summit of Creag Mhór

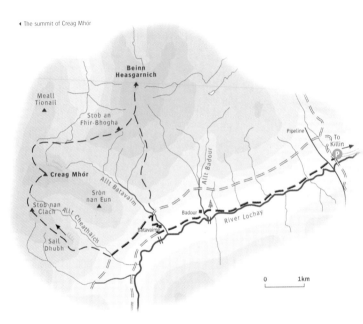

prominent ridge. This is followed easily to the top of Stob nan Clach and down to a bealach on the north side. From the bealach, climb northeast to the summit of Creag Mhór (GR392361) (3h20). Descend westwards for about 300m in distance to avoid cliffs, and then head north towards a bealach shared with Meall Tionail. Drop east to a claggier bealach shared with Beinn Heasgarnich. [Escape: follow the Allt Batavaim back to the track.] Climb the steep west ridge of Sron Tairbh to reach

Stob an Fhir-Bhogha and a high undulating ridge. The summit of Beinn Heasgarnich is 1km to the north (GR414383) (5h40). From the top, return south along the ridge for 500m and then leave the ridge to descend due south through moguls to a flat, boggy area. Continue to descend southwards, keeping east of the Allt Batavaim. Cross the fence by a gate to reach the upper track. Bear west to find the original zigzag approach. Retrace your steps to the floor of the glen (7h). Return to the start.

In its Victorian heyday, Crianlarich was the rail traveller's stop on the way north. It is still a busy place, but Tyndrum is now the hub for visitors to the area and its car parks fill up quickly on good summer days.

With its perfect examples of steep-sided corries and long, defined ridges, the region is particularly attractive to geologists and glaciologists. This area is also known for its mineral deposits. Lead was mined commercially near Tyndrum for 200 years, and the presence of gold has brought prospectors from many countries.

This section includes a circuit of Ben More and Stob Binnein, twin humps that dominate the view when approached from Killin. There are also two shorter routes close to Crianlarich, and an adventurous climb over Ben Lui, a beacon for travellers from Oban. Four routes start near Tyndrum, ranging from a short walk over Beinn Odhar to more demanding full-day treks.

One of the most notable sights in this area has to be the southern flank of Beinn Dorain as it beckons the traveller further, into Lochaber and beyond.

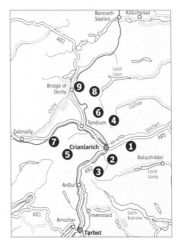

Hills of Crianlarich and Tyndrum

Ben More and Stob Binnein

Ben More Ⓜ(1174m), **Stob Binnein** Ⓜ
(1165m), **Meall na Dìge** (966m)

Walk time 7h Height gain 1400m
Distance 16km OS Map Landranger 51

**A pair of symmetrical mountains that
form a magnificent horseshoe. The final
part of the ridge is hard going but can
be avoided.**

Start from a small layby on the south side
of the A85, 50m west of the bridge where
the Allt Coire Chaorach drops to meet the
River Dochart (GR454276). Climb the
embankment of the layby, cross a low fence
and take a small footpath through a field.
After 150m, you will come to a gate which
leads to a wide forestry track. Follow this
track west for 500m, and turn left onto
a narrower track. This climbs through old
plantation, at first gently and then steeply
when it reaches a burn. The track levels out
higher up, crosses another burn and leaves
the plantation. Climb southwest by a grassy
track to reach a deer fence and gateway,
then follow this fence west towards the
ridge of Sròn nam Fòrsairean. Once on the
ridge, climb southwest either along or just
to the right of the apex: this leads to the
summit and natural rock shelter of Ben
More (GR433245) (3h40). Descend the south
ridge to Bealach-eadar-dha Beinn. From
here, it is an unrelenting climb along the

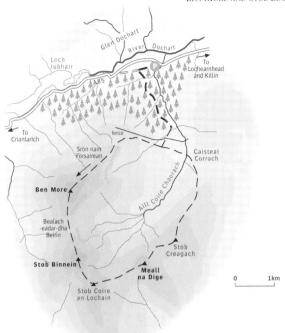

north ridge of Stob Binnein to its summit (GR434227) (4h40). Descend the south ridge, and climb to the top of Stob Coire an Lochain. Do not follow the main path which descends the south ridge: instead cut down ENE, steeply at first, to reach flatter ground and an old wall. [Escape: descend north into the main amphitheatre to join a grassy track by the Allt Coire Chaorach.] Follow the wall which ends as the ridge disappears into folds, making navigation more difficult. Head towards Meall na Dige, which has overhanging cliffs on its west side, and follow the ridge, distinguished by small towers and buttresses, to Stob Creagach. At any convenient point on the far side of Stob Creagach, begin a northwards descent into the corrie to join the Allt Coire Chaorach. Cross the burn and climb north to join the deer fence and gateway. Walk back through the plantation to the start (7h).

◀ The eastern slopes of Ben More with Stob Creagach beyond

79

The Castle and the Twistin Hill

Beinn a'Chroin Ⓜ (940m),
An Caisteal Ⓜ (995m)

Walk time 5h40 Height gain 1000m
Distance 14km OS Map Landranger 50

This route climbs two rocky peaks and descends by a long, curving ridge.

Start from the parking bay on the south side of the A82, 2km south of Crianlarich (GR370240). Go over the stile at the north end of the bay, and cut across a small bog to reach the railway tunnel. Go through this and follow the track southeast, rising gently above the River Falloch. When the track ends after 2km, continue to hug the south bank of the river along a path into Coire Earb. After a further 2km, there is a confluence of two burns. Cross over one and follow the other, which flows from Stob Glas Bheag in the southeast. Climb to reach a plateau and then onto the north ridge of Beinn a'Chroin to meet a twisting path: this keeps the easiest line to the east summit (GR394186) (3h). Descend to the west, and

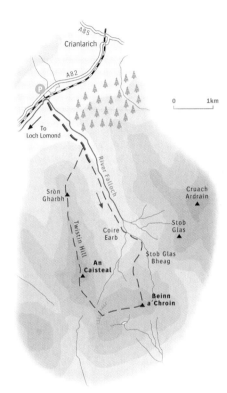

follow the ridge as it climbs and undulates for almost 1km. The descent from here is a little tricky: at the end of the ridge drop south by a compact buttress, then switch back and traverse northwest for 100m. Here, a steep path cuts through crags and down to a bealach. Climb the rocky south ridge of An Caisteal (the Castle) to its summit (GR379193) (4h). Descend via Twistin Hill, the long and narrow north ridge of the mountain: a good path makes for easy walking. Beyond Sròn Gharbh, where the path seems to disappear and the ridge loses definition, bear NNE across grass and bog towards the corner of the plantation to join the track at a gateway. This leads back to the railway (5h40).

Kames and kettles

The effects of glaciology are a common sight in the glens. Between Killin and Tyndrum, there are many examples of sand and gravel mounds known as kames and kettles. As the glaciers scoured the mountains, they broke off rocks and ground them into sediment. The meltwaters carried this downstream and deposited it in subglacial tunnels beneath the ice, sandwiching blocks of ice with layers of debris. When the glacier melted, the compact sediment was sculpted into unusual shapes and ridges whereas the melting ice created the hollows.

◄ Twistin Hill and An Caisteal from Crianlarich

The Hidden Loch and Beinn Chabhair

Beinn Chabhair Ⓜ(933m)

Walk time 6h20 Height gain 1000m
Distance 17km OS Map Landranger 56

An entertaining walk along a complex ridge, returning by a less frequented glen and the Falls of Falloch. Dogs are not allowed on this route.

Start at the entrance to Beinglas farm and camping ground (GR318188). (Park close to Inverarnan.) Follow the helpful instructions for crossing the campsite to meet the West Highland Way. Near the information board, a small zigzag path climbs east by Ben Glas Burn which is at first hidden from view. Higher up, the slope begins to level off and the path deteriorates to bog. Bear northeast across heather to climb Meall Mór nan Eag

and on to the secluded Lochan a'Chaisteil. Continue to follow the ridge over a complex terrain of folds and around or over crags to the steep-sided tower of Stob Creag an Fhithich and beyond. After 2km, the ridge becomes more defined and leads southeast to the summit of Beinn Chabhair (GR368179) (3h40). Descend the south ridge for about 100m to reach a grassy ramp that drops northeast. This can be easily followed towards a wide bealach shared with An Caisteal. Keep above the south side of Allt a'Chuilinn and walk down the glen. Further on at a confluence of two rivers, you will reach the first of many low walls. Continue your descent on the north side of the river, past a ravine and on until you reach a gate. Climb over, and head west for a short distance to reach a track: this is the West Highland Way. Turn southwest onto the excellent path which takes you past the fast-flowing Falls of Falloch and back to the campsite (6h20).

◄ The Allt a'Chuilin with Ben Oss and Beinn Dubhchraig beyond

Ben Challum Circuit

Beinn Chaorach Ⓒ (818m), **Cam Chreag** Ⓒ (884m), **Ben Challum** ⓜ (1025m)

Walk time 7h40 Height gain 1300m
Distance 18km OS Map Landranger 50

An arduous but varied walk around Gleann a'Chlachain. This route involves plenty of ascent.

Start at the car park at the turn-off for Dalrigh (GR343292). Avoid the walk along the busy A82 by taking a small road southeast to a bridge and then a track which bears east to join the main road. Cross, and continue for 400m to a bridge before Auchtertyre. Just before the bridge, take a track which bears steeply uphill on the west side of Gleann a'Chlachain and passes under the railway. After 1.5km, the track crosses a burn and starts to trend west, zigzagging as it climbs towards Beinn Chaorach. Leave the track when the ground levels, and head north. A double line of low wooden posts lead up the broad south ridge of Beinn Chaorach to the summit (GR359328) (2h40). Follow the posts down gentle ground to a rounded and boggy bealach, and then climb northeast. The summit of Cam Chreag is not far behind a line of crags and is scattered with perched blocks. From the summit, bear southeast over undulating ground. Before reaching the end of the ridge, descend south across

grassland to Bealach Ghlas Leathaid.
Ascend Ben Challum by the northwest
ridge. A section of slabs about midway can
be scrambled or passed on the east side.
Further up, a broken tower is best avoided
on the west side. The higher north summit
is reached first (GR386322) (5h40). From
here, drop to a bealach and ascend the
rocky fin to the lower summit. Descend
the broad southwest ridge along a
fenceline: this soon reaches a flat
area with a crag on each side.
Continue to follow the fence on
its east side over a knoll, and
watch for a stile soon after.
Cross to the other side, and
follow an intersecting fence
west over bog. This drops
quickly towards the glen.
Another fence blocks
access to the river:
follow it southwest
through two gates
and over a stile.
Cross the river by
the footbridge to join
the original track. (7h40).

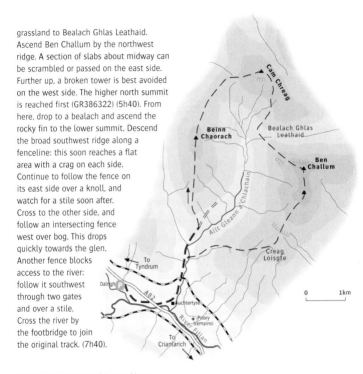

Saint Fillan's Priory and Bannockburn

Saint Fillan was an 8th-century Irish monk who spent most of his life in Scotland, becoming
Abbot of St Andrews and founder of a place of worship near Auchtertyre. Following his
defeat at the Battle of Methven, Robert the Bruce received shelter there and, in gratitude,
founded a Priory on the site. On the eve of the Battle of Bannockburn in 1314, he received
a relic of St Fillan which was said to have contributed to his famous victory. A number of
other artefacts relating to the Saint are on display at the Folklore Centre in Killin.

◀ Ben Challum from Glen Lochay

Ben Oss and Beinn Dubhchraig

Beinn Dubhchraig ⓜ (978m),
Ben Oss ⓜ (1029m)

Walk time 8h Height gain 1100m
Distance 20km OS Map Landranger 50

**A good route through Caledonian pine,
climbing two high peaks and returning
beneath the flanks of Ben Lui.**

Start at the car park at the turn-off for
Dalrigh (GR343292). Follow a small road
southeast to a bridge over the River
Cononish. Cross the bridge, and turn right
onto the small grassy track. After 1km, pass
over a railway bridge and leave the track

immediately after to follow a path
southwest for 300m across open ground.
Cross the Allt Gleann Auchreoch by a
footbridge, and take a good path which
trends SSW through old pine and starts to
follow the Allt Coire Dubhchraig on its
north bank. The path winds up through the
forest and over two stiles before emerging
on to open moorland. Continue alongside
the burn, past several waterfalls and
through a wide corrie to reach the top of
the ridge by two small lochans. The summit
of Beinn Dubhchraig, with its views down
Loch Lomond, is a short walk to the

southeast (GR307255) (3h40). Return to the lochans and bear west to a bealach. Contour southwest at this level under a knoll to reach a wide, grassy gully. Climb the gully, and join the ridge which is easily followed to the summit of Ben Oss (GR287253) (5h20). Descend southwest in a wide arc to reach a bealach above

Coire Laoigh. Drop to the north side of the bealach to a burn. Follow this on the west bank beneath the imposing bulk of Ben Lui. Where the waters turn east, head northwest to reach and ford the Allt an Rund. This leads to a track which keeps high above the River Cononish and takes you back to the start (8h).

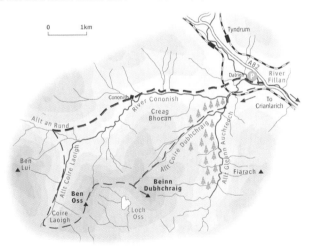

The Brooch of Lorne

In a Franciscan priory in Dumfries in 1306, Robert the Bruce murdered his rival John 'Red' Comyn, whom he suspected of shifting allegiance to the court of Edward I of England. Comyn was a nephew of the MacDougall clan chief and in retaliation the Bruce was attacked while travelling through Dalrigh in Strath Fillan. Robert escaped but the Brooch of Lorne, a crystal mounted in silver and edged with pearls, was ripped from his plaid and is still in the possession of the MacDougall clan.

◀ Ben Oss from Beinn Dubhchraig

The Mines of Odhar

Beinn Odhar ⓒ (901m)

Walk time 4h Height gain 700m
Distance 8km OS Map Landranger 50

**A pleasant half-day walk with an
initial steep section. This route starts
from Tyndrum, following the West
Highland Way.**

Start on the west side of the bridge in
Tyndrum at a signpost for the West
Highland Way (GR328306). Take a road on
the west bank of the river heading north:
this soon becomes a track and, after about
1km, reaches a bridge and gate. Just after
the gate, leave the track and bear eastwards
towards the corner of a large plantation.
Cross the Crom Allt and climb steeply
eastwards alongside the forest. After 150m
of height gain, where the terrain steepens
further, take a rising traverse northeast to
reach a line of shattered crags. These can
be passed at the northernmost end. From
here, walk easily up to a double line of low
fencing at the bealach that Beinn Odhar
shares with Meall Buidhe. The ridge
continues northwards over several false

tops before trending northwest. Pass a small lochan and continue to the summit of Beinn Odhar (GR338339) (2h40). Descend steeply southwards over scree to a lochan where the ground levels off. Drop down on the east side of the fence along the wide south ridge. About halfway down, this passes the ruined shelters and rejected stone of former mine workings. Continue south to the railway bridge, and follow the West Highland Way back to the start (4h).

Lead and gold

Lead ore was mined in this area – 10,000 tons from 1741 to 1862 and 1916 to 1925 – and the remains of several small lead mines can be seen on the slopes of Beinn Odhar. The nearby settlement of Tyndrum was the centre of a brief gold rush in the 19th century and another in the early 1990s when the Cononish vein was discovered. The fever has since died down, but it remains one of the most significant gold deposits in Scotland and attracts many keen prospectors.

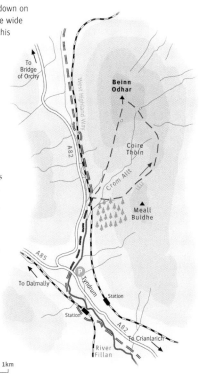

0   1km

◄ Beinn Odhar from the West Highland Way

Ben Lui

Beinn a'Chleibh ⓜ (916m),
Ben Lui ⓜ (1130m)

Walk time 4h40 Height gain 1100m
Distance 10km OS Map Landranger 50

**A short mountaineering expedition with
some exciting scrambling. The route
also involves a river crossing and some
potentially deep bog. In winter this is
a serious undertaking.**

Start from a hidden parking area on the
road to Dalmally (GR238278). Take the path
which leads south to the river, and then
follow it downstream for 300m until you are
opposite a railway bridge. Wade across the
river here, and then pass under the railway
to gain a well-defined path through the
forest. Keeping to the east side of a burn,

follow the path upstream to a confluence.
Cross the first burn to follow another more
southerly path, often through deep mud.
This emerges from the trees into an arena
between the peaks of Beinn a'Chleibh and
Ben Lui. For some adventure, climb steep
slopes southwest towards Stob Dubh, the
rocky northwest buttress of Beinn a'Chleibh.
This is crossed by a prominent grassy ramp
at half height. Traverse airily along this until
you are about 200m beyond a rocky gully.
From here, climb steep grassy steps (at a
40-degree angle) to the top of Stob Dubh.
[Variant: from the edge of the forest,
contour WSW below Stob Dubh to find and
ascend the west ridge to the top.] Continue
southeast over more grass to the summit of
Beinn a'Chleibh (GR250256) (2h20).

Descend a good path WNW over rocky terrain to a bealach. [Escape: a path from the middle of the bealach leads northwest into Fionn Choirein and back to the forest.] Climb the long southwest ridge of Ben Lui by a path (scree and boulders disguise the line higher up) to gain the summit (GR266263) (3h40). Care should be taken around the steep northeast corrie. Descend NNW along a very exposed ridge, negotiating several rocky steps to reach gentler ground. Bear westwards down grassy slopes to the forest, and take the original track back to the start (4h40).

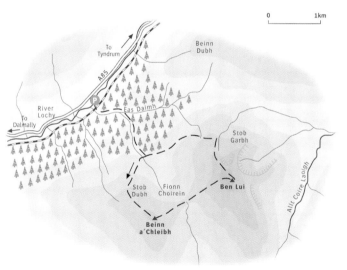

Tyndrum

At the junction of three routes, to the south, west and north, Tyndrum grew as a meeting place for cattle drovers on their way to the markets at Crieff and Falkirk. The name means 'house on the ridge' as it lies in a bleak moorland landscape on the watershed between east and west. Nowadays, it is a welcome fuel stop for walkers on the West Highland Way as well as for motorists and coach parties.

◄ Strath Fillan with Ben Lui and Beinn Chuirn in the distance

Circuit of Gleann Cailliche

Beinn Mhanach ⓜ (953m),
Beinn Achaladair ⓜ (1038m),
Beinn a'Chreachain ⓜ (1081m)

Walk time 7h40 Height gain 1400m
Approach and return 2h40 bike or 5h walk
Distance 20km + 18km approach and return
OS Maps Landranger 50 and 51

**A long and varied walk into remote
country with views over Rannoch Moor
and the peaks of Glen Lyon. Use of a
bike is advised for the approach.**

Start at the top of the pass between
Tyndrum and Bridge of Orchy (GR330325).
[Variant: start at Tyndrum and walk the
West Highland Way.] Take the track
signposted for Glen Lyon north along the
railway to Auch Gleann. When you reach a
bridge, turn right to pass under the viaduct
and continue northeast along the Allt
Kinglass. The track fords the river several
times, passes a sheep enclosure and splits
below Beinn a'Chùirn. Take the track on the
right, and climb towards Srath Tarabhan.
Bikes can be left at the water catchment:
walk times begin at this point. Climb
steeply by a fence on the east side of a
burn to gain height quickly. As it
approaches a bealach, leave the fence and
trend east to the summit of Beinn Mhanach.
Return to the bealach, and descend
northwest by the fence to another bealach.
Climb west to join the long ridge of Beinn
Achaladair and the top of its southern peak.
Follow the ridge northwards to the summit
(GR344432) (3h40). A winding path
descends steeply on the east side before
rising to the top of Meall Buidhe. The route

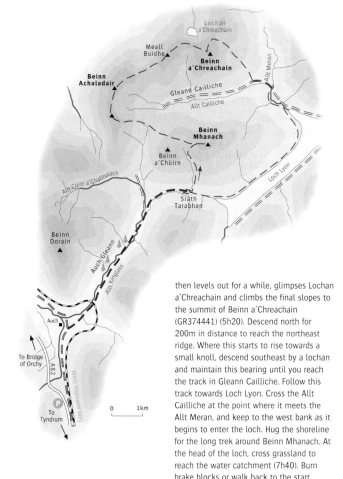

then levels out for a while, glimpses Lochan a'Chreachain and climbs the final slopes to the summit of Beinn a'Chreachain (GR374441) (5h20). Descend north for 200m in distance to reach the northeast ridge. Where this starts to rise towards a small knoll, descend southeast by a lochan and maintain this bearing until you reach the track in Gleann Cailliche. Follow this track towards Loch Lyon. Cross the Allt Cailliche at the point where it meets the Allt Meran, and keep to the west bank as it begins to enter the loch. Hug the shoreline for the long trek around Beinn Mhanach. At the head of the loch, cross grassland to reach the water catchment (7h40). Burn brake blocks or walk back to the start.

◄ Coire an Lochain on Beinn a'Chreachain

The Twins of Orchy

Beinn Dorain Ⓜ (1076m),
Beinn an Dòthaidh Ⓜ (1004m)

Walk time 5h40 Height gain 1100m
Distance 12km OS Map Landranger 50

**A route which climbs the striking
Beinn Dorain and its twin, Beinn an
Dòthaidh, with a short steep section
in descent.**

Start from the Bridge of Orchy Hotel
(GR297396). Cross the A82 and walk to the
station, then pass under the railway to
reach a track. Bear north for just a few
metres to join another track which leads
directly to radio masts. This track continues
as a path on the south bank of the Allt
Coire an Dothaidh to the steep-walled Coire

an Dòthaidh. From here, climb east to the
bealach and its cairn (GR325398). Beinn
Dorain looks a different mountain from this
viewpoint: a mass of complex ridges and
buttresses. Climb a path steeply to the
south. Soon the terrain flattens, and the
path weaves around a lochan before
continuing southwards. After another steep
but short ascent, the path splits. Take the
left fork to follow the north ridge to the
summit (GR325378) (3h). [Variant: the right
fork makes for an adventurous traverse of
the western side of Beinn Dorain before the
path fades: from here continue directly to
the top.] Return to the bealach. For Beinn an
Dòthaidh, ascend a path northwest to flatter,
boggier ground. Keeping to the west side of

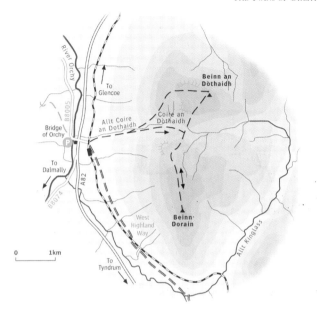

a burn, ascend the higher east summit (GR332408) (4h20). Care should be taken as there are steep cliffs in many directions. Follow the summit ridge west to the lower peak, and then trend WSW down gentle slopes to a plateau. Aim for the far

southwest edge of the plateau to descend directly towards Bridge of Orchy. This descent is very steep at first (keep right to avoid bands of rock), but soon eases. Drop to the burn, cross the water and follow the path to the start point (5h40).

The Bard of Glen Orchy

'Twas health and strength, 'twas life and joy, to wander freely there / To drink at the fresh mountain stream, to breathe the mountain air'. Duncan Bàn MacIntyre or 'Fair Duncan' (1724-1812) was an illiterate forester whose unsentimental poems in Gaelic made him famous throughout Scotland. MacIntyre's best known poem was 'In Praise of Ben Dorain', about the hill where he lived and worked for much of his life. There are two monuments to him: one at Dalmally overlooking Loch Awe and the other marking his grave in Edinburgh's Greyfriars Kirkyard.

◀ Beinn Dorain from Creag Mhór

Index

Ⓜ **Munros** are mountains in Scotland above 914m (3000ft). (Named after Sir Hugh Munro who compiled the first list in 1891.)

Ⓒ **Corbetts** are peaks between 762m and 914m (2500ft and 3000ft) which have a drop of at least 152m (500ft) on all sides. (Named after John Corbett who drew up the list and made the first ascent.)